T0308996

Kluge: A Meditation
and other works

Books by Brian Kim Stefans

What Is Said to the Poet Concerning Flowers (2006)
Before Starting Over: Selected Interviews and Essays 1994-2005 (2006)
Fashionable Noise: On Digital Poetics (2003)
Angry Penguins (2000)
Gulf (1998)
Free Space Comix (1998)

Kluge: A Meditation

and other works

Brian Kim Stefans

Roof Books
New York

Copyright 2007 by Brian Kim Stefans
ISBN 13: 978-1-931824-24-8
ISBN 10: 1-931824-24-X
Library of Congress Control Number: 2007921408

Book Design: Arras Media
Author photograph: Brooke Bocast

ACKNOWLEDGEMENTS AND NOTES
"The Slush of Meaning" appeared in *The Brown Literary Review* and "Five Coiled Stanzas" was published by D Press in "Poetry Pow Wow." "Five Finger Exercises" and "Kluge: A Meditation" are the texts for electronic poems which appear at www.arras.net/kluge. The second season of "Kluge" is based on Robert Coover's short story "The Iron Poker" in *Pricksongs and Descants* and takes many lines directly from it. The third season is based on the life of H.P. Lovecraft and takes many lines from his letters and his short story "Dagon." Alexandra Sears' short story "Lentils" provides much of the text of Sonia's letter. A plethora of borrowed texts appear in "Blabbermouth Night," most notably the entirety of "I hear a banging on the door of the night" by Jack Spicer. "Where Stones Gather" had a staged reading at the Ontological Hysteric Theater in "Play on Words: A Poets and Theater Festival" (May 12 2006), curated by Lee Ann Brown, Corina Copp and Tony Torn. Directed by Tony Torn, it starred Kate Valk as Kate Valk, Angelica Torn as Hanna Schygulla and Charles Bernstein as Jason Robards. "Summary" is derived from Kenneth Goldsmith's *Soliloquy*—a book composed of the entirety of what he said for a week—and "auto-summarized" in Microsoft Word to be two percent of its original length. A short version of "Summary" was performed at St. Mark's Poetry Project with Alan Licht on guitar (audio at www.ubu.com). "Sehnsucht" was composed with the aid of a computer in 1998. My thanks to the editors of these journals and websites, and to the organizers of these events.

This book is for my friends. "To be a jarring and a dissonant thing"—Coleridge

ROOF BOOKS are distributed by
Small Press Distribution
1341 Seventh Avenue
Berkeley, CA 94710-1403
Phone orders: 800-869-7553
spdbooks.org

This book was made possible, in part, with public funds from the New York State Council on the Arts, a state agency.

NYSCA

ROOF BOOKS
are published by
The Segue Foundation
303 East 8th Street
New York, NY 10009
seguefoundation.com

CONTENTS

❦

kludge or kluge (klo͞oj)
n. Slang

1. A system, especially a computer system, that is constituted of poorly matched elements or of elements originally intended for other applications.
2. A clumsy or inelegant solution to a problem.

THE FURTHER ADVENTURES OF OEDIPUS MESS IN THE COUNTESS SECOND'S FLAT

"suggestive pix on greige"—Ashbery

(no pacing)

"Gone to Croatoan"—humming a big city of scars, nothing to loathe about it now—
crawling on glass but the norms of feudal life pull up in a leased Lamborghini—we smoke,
lambaste government, gel our Mohawks, though attentively persist

—predatory TV—AT THE EDGE OF WINDERNESS—shades of "Crimson and Clover"
starring Malcolm McDowell as Claudius, Rimbaud Archangel filmed by Gus Van Sant—no—
filmed by Guy Maddin, yes.

"poetic thinking" (love—death—sex—life—anger—etc., no—

and agrees—now shades of Icarian transport—as pollen-style production proffers cheap substitutes:
Cote d'Ivoire for Ivory Coast, soy dogs for Polish "Derma-Thrash" films,
theta-axis limbering—shackles of liberalism—almost none of them caught in the exact same
        moods

—the backend whiplash of these catastrophes continues to humble.

Redolent of some revolutionary Spring with the body squads
—So that you and I were reduced to mere observers /
analyzing our hate

꧅

I don't need a lover

who looks like that

—rather like criticism—in the battery of cello notes).

This Benny Goodman tune piercing my ear
—on hold with HIP, waiting for my "Advocate,"
that advances me three minutes into my—you can read about it in the obit—

preternatural dotage—chatterbox nostalgic, wearing a polystyrene bathing cap—right out of
           Grey
Gardens—not quite toothless and wise (vegetable, in fact)
—ungrounded in this plinth of mores (but I was not the first one to think of it).

"I wire up your fingers, and chase you right out
of my bra"—now I think that's Natalie Merchant at the other end (hardly my Advocate
but she's been known to speak up for the entire Sub-limnal continent

and that's just through her pretty, multitasking
press agent.)
—skipping on rusty toe thimbles preaching development arrest to the perverse.

We get to hip-hop—I'm being thanked (thrashed) now for holding,
but am not holding out for the fateful edits that "blend together your lives
and mine"—no

           —colon-precipitated misanthropy
           —Lovecraftian "materialism"
           —Harvard law chests animated calling it Right
           —shiny immortals letting the tie down—the hair, in freedom to climb!—to *le peuple*

We're getting nowhere—but with you it's ok because "you" in this case
is the proto bling bling album of 1981, *Paradise Theater* by Styx
—"Tonight's the night
                    we make Listerine…"

—and though you're not my Advocate,
you sound like you really care.

—"gentile mix"—optimism (Disney)
—the travails of Zoloft / Cerebral Hemorrhage Village released on Thai DVD
—THEY'VE CALLED ME BACK TO DEATH—with director's commentary—Finding it

so much more charming to be physically entwined
                                        with SPECTACULAR forms of government

—I missed out on dancing
with Jenelle last night
for fear of my shoes falling

off
—because of these asides—eight young girls abducted
from sitcoms, transferred here to stand in line and *just wear thin*)—JUST
        WAITING FOR THE BANDWIDTH.

If there were a surgical procedure I could use to improve this, I'd do it in a second.

(I'm David Lupescu.)

～

I woke up because my dentures were dirty
and all the thinking was like 1976
—Would that were There suburbs are settings of richness, you ask,

—even the high-falutin monastic bidness of the poetry of Denis Roche can't keep the acci-
            dents out of
this poem; moving to the left
margin, moving to the other, moving back—theme songs and anthems.—

(my questions seem irritable, if antique, and she hears me
somehow in L.A. / Mt. Taishan—"candescent in mist"—(obvious parallelism there)—

Where the marvelous and the profane mingled with drawing-room ease,
you found several of their celebrities
                            in studied *dishabille*
—they meld the big toe with the longest—and amble like a wounded John Cleese

—methods approved by the Heterodoxy Hierophants
of Iowa
—mentioned in the *Encyclopedia of American Writers*, featured in the PMLA)—in air-
            conditioned omniscience—the breath sometimes ice.

Banality: this is what he writes.
howling pregnant Stats

JUST LIKE YOU SAID—KEVIN Things were better in 1603.
—just long enough to tell me I belong neither in nor out—
flowing-bearded prophet on jaundiced 34th / Among the Powers and reruns of *Dallas*—
   survival of the glibbest.

Gump: "I'm probably the easiest guy on earth, but I got this *calling*."
Abba: FREEDOM IS FORCED SOUP.
(no heart)

—He woke up in a house full of people.
—And did the whole-weight-of-the-world jabberwalk in streetwise Aramaic
for sexual favors.)
     I just sat down and wrote this.

Then I argue "I *am*,"
and they move in to find out!

It—they didn't know what *it* was
—grabbed the baby with eight retractable tentacles and she disappeared beneath the cast iron
        surface of the partly submerged vessel—in 1888 in 1999 in 2001 in 2999 in Flor-
        ence in Guatemala—never to be seen again by the D Celeb contingent
—at least until the Meher Baba theme park came to Charlottesville again. / Couldn't we

have relied, couldn't aspire?

                           I've got myself in my pocket
though had to hit "resend" 73 times—just to get settled—just to get *convinced*.

My love was for them who had failed to complete

even one significant sentence
—not just proof of honesty and a signed declaration of negative intent—*that's* not it
—when she accuses me of simply being rebarbative and having crystals of coke crowding my
        nostrils—call and response (suckass and SHOWDOWN).
                                  Writing

like a cavity—how to wake one to the specificity and damage
—who—spruced by Krispies
—my tense is to believe him outright

with the "gift economy" pulling red caps over Black personal grammar
becoming grids and another city's grinds Well—I still have my De Kooning to aspire to.

✎

Strident?
—across the green morning lawns,
sort of French, with sibilant *cocks*... though I be a moisture   blue as puke

—I know what you're thinking:
>   a hypertrophied paragraph "obsessively" teased out Thomas Bernhard-style for an
>   impressive debut volume

—the That which has not been Experienced; yet
—it makes me think of HOME.

Pat Robertson: "death to Chavez."
—with a cursed lorgnette—"let us hurt" Friday at 7—"trial commences"—click to make
a tax-deductible resolution. /
>   But I have forgotten that you are about to call.

—He wondered aloud before memory (madeleines) plummeted—lo Bruno S.
hero to several hundred goat-bearded NYU film school nerds
who couldn't tell a Stallone
>   from a Leonardo di Caprio—no.
>   Bruno calls.
>   —carrying what looked like a pig fetus under one arm

—it is an advancement on pure self-knowledge as it posits quite clearly the "other"—
>   Afro-Acadian syllogisms
>   and Swedish igneous rocks. Yes

—couldn't such disparagement of traditional cultural "perspectivalism"
be pimped?

—into a *spiritualism*
—some Planeat Repo for the denizens of Williamsburg
to—"convulsively"—DO/traffick—
>   BASTA

෨

Partly to displace

the erotism of the screens:
when an onlooker might be susceptible to masculine excess,
you pull on the choker, bark sexual commands

—blur with vampirish affect
the temptations of synaesthetic panic.

Damned
difficult
art
       of good

prose.

All the Ashberites and anti-Ashberites were warring in the main traffic circle of Latterday
        Saint City; Gerard de Nerval's strychnine dreambook
—under the dark of night, the moon tonguing the surge protector—tattered and swearing,
        swept by on a leash,
—one suffered for the bourgeois toe-hold to reassert itself, every actor streaming by so
        quickly—a "quickly clearing night" (seeing painting by Boccioni),

—all proper, objective angles jettisoned for the insurrection, as if spontaneous debt relief weren't
        enough
for the E Generation—or they were simply taking themselves too seriously;
—then, basking in the glow of Hi Facility, frisking the Casbah night for goo-gone Swatches
        and Jubilees,—which is why this became

political:
feral teenagers
in high-saturation tan-lines, Raybans setting the norms

for the slowly, but surely, fossilizing—
Premieres of Change
grinning through silicon ass-cheeks

—pimples just back from the lab (negative)
—and with an addiction to protein bars / Icelandic Techno
—outré blandishments—somewhat patterned after the Greasy Kid, but his Red health
        spurned it, with a variety of techniques that, a pantomime

played out one's singular fantasies in private, fertile arrangements
—and after that the
sleep.

❦

COSMIC SNIGGLY
Are you sometimes completely unable to enter the spirit of things?
(finally,
        Nietzschean New York!)

I'll let the manner of the Mod with the coifed pate brush away my doubts—a shotgun angel:
      exotic salads hurled by painted eyelids.
Would that were the suburbs are settings of richness,
—converting deficient sublimes—into high-priced tenement lofts

—so that the soldiers paintball in Il Duce's palaces
—and for the rest
dots.

THE FURTHER ADVENTURES OF OEDIPUS MESS IN THE COUNTESS SECOND'S FLAT

—A history of textual torsions: but they couldn't call up
the temerity of youth any more than I could excoriate
the pace of physical contacts, or recall the quality of those doe-like legs, twenty years past
      louche touches,

—fishhooks in every eye—sans insurrectional *hacks*—Perhaps my failure as a karaoke singer in
      middle-age Protestant "geisha" dens could eliminate these
Senatorial impulses.

(Comedy: all sorts of deceptions.)

A LITTLE GREEN MARTIAN
To grease the wheels of steel
He made some joke about how *A Streetcar Named Desire* was written about him.

꙳

(we
relax, medically disparate, like a shattered Calder—"situation standby" as the sump moans
staring into the blue eyes, into Learning—leaning into the wheel, when national motivation is
        winnowing, as Oprah's

Geiger
counter
clicks, as the cat…

manipulated by visions of lake scenery and matters of intestinal import
—excuse me—I'm having one of those "Café Bustelo moments"—that solidifies opinions—
        that stokes piss—
(a poet with foresight optimizing the pineal gland for Desert Sputter…)—the latex

concoctions of the Stylist as he ribbons by the wharves,
the fraught air of the Controversialist blooming in seven boroughs
toss up palpable, if impressionistic, digits
                             —in time

the dust of satisfactory explosions)

Pulsing music
        —some trailer park accusations
—MFA-brand camera angles
            —and now some audience help:

Is a word primed for lecture phallus Roman complex (hence) replication—anon allure—through
        the umpteenth Netwerk with dog names—names have dogs—and dogs have names—so
        doth—

is anyone playing as honestly as I?

That's when a blending of proof and honesty does not offer up
the felicities of prose—and banter, which I like,
is leveled to the pro-forma fantasy of emancipatory cribs

—"Large Marge" for the Cheeseworthy tip—that's to say, literary dynamism was lost on these
        kids,
schooled in epochal parataxis—those promised pages of cataclysmic
"counter socialization" debated and deleted—key tones after keystroke laid end-to-
        ampersand—

(no conclusion)

⁊

by the time I'd read the phrases "like so many Lucky Pierres," "like so many indigenous histo-
ries," and "like so many empty calories"
—I was beginning to wonder where Chaz put his anatomy of associative thought / I
failed to be annoyed—yes

until a certain eco-satiety set in:

knowing the family
of my customs,

When it downgraded to a domestic mysticism—the field of my interests blurred into so much eth-
nic hype—jazz voices festooned over systematic *détournement* of whizzing dental surgery
samples—and a Bollywood six-pack of Botox
when it quiets down—my depression increases in tactile, yet affordable, increments—such that inner
logic of psychic attrition is countered by monthly cycles of fashion-conscious libido—she
asked me to play triangle in her band, Plug N The Philomaths—I agree—plausibly vernal,
fleshy (profane)
—then—when the naively prolific accuse me of a lack of imagination—"Jesuitical caffeine"—how
make a reliable *business* of it?—with tats, provided I could croon like an Asbury Park Klaus
Nomi

also

When ,

when juiced in alembic straits—they falter in catcalls of doting mothers and bureaucratic
difficulties among the nuances of a seemingly intractable acculturation.
, as they were unable to write any good pornography.

When they, the demons flourishes of words suffused with storms

and never proven born

a talent /
with clamps and scissors

Dancing, dancing like this.

The monks will rotate in their prayer wheels, the collegiates in their fun,
and the awards will go to the most unlikely couplings;—question being asked:
Can I read this in a public of the "unofficial"?

Anywhere was the location to start interrogating
this celestial (cholesterol) philosophy—the PhD's
WMD.—

cloacally distributed Spoonerisms unscrewing the brass daddy-arm of the Shriner Nationalists
—mentions in thick journals bee-lined to stud-prone—nipples and hagiographies
—as we pirated the newsprint from Italian *Yahoo!* and called it "copy"—

the sentence like a gash—that bleeds both ways.

FIVE FINGER PIECES

short poems for digital works

❧

To Error

1.
Some penmanship resembles fallen hair.

2.
Idi in Africa assembles a bowl of air.

3.
Bees make hives into a simple airport.

4.
I eat peas as abler edibles dissemble.

Winter Was Hard

A. Manon couldn't play that evocative music.
B. Please erase me after you have read this.
C. There are odd children in the playground.
D. Bad karma cannot be good for your breath.

Crappy drumbeat over chinkachink guitars.
Please remember me after going from here.
Winter was hard but felt like wet sponge.
Stress dangles its seductive wares ahead.

Is this a fadeout or was the plug pulled?
Please forget what you read on this page.
My sexless neighbor records my movements.
Bad hamburger cannot be good for your id.

Benny couldn't muster much gizmo alchemy.
Please absorb me after you power me down.
Garbage is picked up each Friday morning.
Anxiety introduced me to midnight sweats.

Betty Boop voice over ambient razorblade.
Please disturb me if you find I'm asleep.
After mass the trees start dressing down.
Bad hungers cannot be good for your pets.

Jordan couldn't recover the sonic thread.
Please ignore me if it's very repetitive.
The accents suggest a failed tracheotomy.
Fear curls up in the cupboard like a cat.

Loops of dreamy static above femmy howls.
Please revise me if you can do it better.
Chugachug sounds from below could be sex.
Bad puns cannot be good for the cerebrum.

Alex couldn't sustain the skronk nirvana.
Please disabuse me if you know I'm wrong.
Tangerine to baby shit green to blue sky.
Is that ringing in my ears cancer or god?

They play in sync and call it revolution.
Please remind me why you are touching me.
Spanish grocery sells the cheap espresso.
Bad coffee cannot be good for the libido.

Gina couldn't emulate the low-fi sublime.
Please reject me after plagiarizing this.
Spring will arrive on sturdy gilt ankles.
Hope festers like a wound that will heal.

A Car Drives to Rome

for Rachel Szekely

A car drives to Rome, a prayer has a theory.
A pigeon has a stoop, a girl talks to dolls.
A man talks to whales, a gun has a holster.
A park feels like home, a pigeon walks to Wales.

A style has a practice, a beer drowns a fish.
A program has no nuts, a deer freezes in headlights.
A hairstyle has roots, a towel dries apples.
A practice has nurses, a fish drowns in beer.

A sport has performers, a man buries a cab.
A spy signals a submarine, an old man has smut.
A parody has laughter, a mullah eats bread.
A judge settles arguments, a movie depicts a sport.

A bastard suns in the park, a toad has farts.
A baby has warts, a photographer peers at flowers.
A prison receives communion, a boy has nuts.
A hawk spirals above the sun, a car drives to Rome.

The Vulgar Muse(Five Coiled Stanzas)

1.

There are scandals in the soup:
a stew of lewd, dramatic coups.
The same can be said of virgins
urged to scoop up aged mermans.

2.

Are we not men, or are we Devo?
Are we not women (ditto, Devo?)
Fervid zeroes preen like heroes
(Neros, all) transfixed by Emo.

3.

She toyed with her hair, mussed
by acid breath inside the mall.
Supercalifragilistic, she said,
There's nothing like halitosis.

4.

It's Carrot Top versus Al Roker
all day, all day. Give me Empty
V. (Vision.) It's like Yoda say
-s: *I sense much fear in you...*

5.

There are lechers in the group:
lushes, loafers, leechers, too.
They try to get a fuck from you
sucking the hock from Truthful.

The Slush of Meaning

after Noam Chomsky

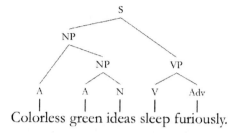

Colorless green ideas sleep furiously.

Colorless green ideas sleep furiously.
Sticky oleaginous memoirs murder affably.
Obsolete futuristic psalms spar quizzically.
Patternless checkered plantains fart sideways.

Virtuoso inept atheists excommunicate charismatically.
Plump boney sandals parse ahead.
Powerless manhandling whispers deafen preferentially.
Teutonic Chinese igloos incubate wisely.

Ineffable aggravating shrubs leer tactfully.
Autocratic indentured slaves unionize individually.
Arthritic nimble logarithms amplify quietly.
Colorless green ideas sleep furiously.

GROUND SEQUENCE, ETC.

Song (from "The Media")

after Medea

Kate, a model, conceals something in her hands.

Kate:
Often I'm the last to know when it's time to work or time to relax.
I usually only act those things, it's not something I ever control.
Jack, he's done so much for me, and made me more than I ever thought.
He's made of this homely trailer park girl a woman the press adore.
Even fear, sometimes, I'm afraid, yes, when they think I'm in a *mood*.

But, but this can't go on, I know that this can't, this can't go on.
I know what Jack is hiding—not *hiding*, for in fact he tells me all.
That is his motive for honesty—to remind me that he's free, I not.
But this can't, this just can't go on, it's not in my deepest core.
I cannot play the *other* woman, I cannot be the star orbiting alone.

When I am the face in one of his photographs, I am white as an albino.
I am delicate as a porcelain china doll, or languorous as an anaconda.
But inside I am black, black, and hard as granite, and tightly wound.
I can see the things that are happening to me, but I make no sound.
Like him, in service to art, I retreat—inside—stare blindly out.

But, but this can't go on, I know that this can't, this can't go on.
I know that he has a soul, but it is divided between—oh, is it *two*?
There is so much enervating doubt not knowing where his passions lie,
If his words to me are eruptions of love, or rehearsals to televise.
Do I only live in *his* photographs—can I choose when to live or die?

(Suddenly, her wistful mood disappears.)

That's why I've devised this cutting tool, easy to conceal in my palm!
One little slip of this wire saw, and his little pecker will be mine!
I'm going to get that lively Johnson, boy-o, and feed it to the dogs!
Jack won't be able to *jack* any more—he'll be talking like a dwarf!
Next he comes to venerate *me*, I'll reply with caresses—and cut it off!

(Afraid she gave the game away, concealing the saw) Oops!

Poem

Hal-
f the
shit
is real-
ly
bad.
Badly.

*

Madonna doesn't
wanna be the
"Maternal Girl"
'cause they are all un-

happy, chil-
dren of married
parents, and
divorce should be

socialized:
all parents should
fly, frank and
merry, undepartmental-

ized, solo
into TV night
like a pop star
admired from afar.

*

In his
impatience (he was
really
angry)—

stocked up
on reds
of wine
and blood—

he
flew! (ar-

rogantly,
but like an

ar-
row, bursting)
to no
new know-

ledge.

*

I can't imagine,
child-like, in bed
to rise, run
fathomless

rose clouds, crystal
veins split,
as factual as
arithmetic

curses for cities,
sonorous, snot
blood dried
hysteric

like a Christian
on methane,
or an acrobat,
or an androgyne.

*

The penis
is presumed innocent
until slightly guilty.

Little Guts

It's lower in the House,
it's higher on the Wall,

oh, who will come to tell them
when I have told them all?

Because I have got a hemorrhoid
and am in another war.

      *

God bless the husband
God bless the children
God bless the nation
God bless the filling station

God bless Gerard Manley Hopkins
God bless diseases
God bless this mission
God bless your sessions

God bless dissenters
God bless Prime Ministers
God bless predicates
God bless bleacher creatures

God bless your senses
Centuries of it
Uncoiling in chip sets
Which are now inexpensive

      *

By the power of whimsy learning
to speak, by the
gusts of wind implicit
in just the wrong words.

We can just transcribe
and be alive
as artists of doggerel
that is "material."

But I talks to You just as

I do with you,
in variable peace, and
physical integrity.

*

1 2 buckle my shoe
3 4 buckle my shoe
5 6 buckle my shoe
7 8 buckle my shoe

*

Who isn't sleeping
is standing.

Dull radar.
Little guts.

A Skein

So this is how it all
starts—grumps
    (first ur-syllable, spit
       from primordial
slime, excavating
from the
     mind, numero uno infinitesimal
        digit) then
love, which needs no syntax.
No therapy makes that connection.

Our Trek

Garbo to home base:
trekking somnolent
amid the defining disgrace
of the historical moment.

Lou Grant to Mary:
rocket's profoundly
tracking rightward, scarily
circling roundly.

Captain Kangaroo to
Geraldo Rivera: sinking
ships to rescue
still, in private thinking.

Kirk to Spock: specks
pummel the windshield
spidering these fallopian treks;
they will not yield.

Elementary Buddhism

Strike a match, a pun in the wind, the window pain. The stitch elegant against splitting, a suture, a way of sitting, a winning. Boy, they say, play play until the tremors go away: I don't know, don't care to know, now. This is the wind speaking—echoing, state to state. This is the crime oblivious, the fright elastic, and signs curve me ever inward, puck's balance, talentless. These chords of connective tissue that I ordered in the mail, wrapped in preserving plastic, starved in their institution, pronouncing its final syllables of revolution—with a doctorate or a general acceptance, within doctrine, these chords are not vibrating, they've stopped, placating. And all the truths are relevant dragging a desperate mile through bogs of shit and temperaments that argue for, or against, style. These truths we've come to believe are hardly material, but only gaseous, or like some lump sum that never approaches, from its third realm, the physical. In its condom: striking a match, a pun. The raw, the unrefined find again in the cooked mind, a way to sleep, slip happy domestic in a challenging way, a map against all becoming. Calm, he wipes it down, clean again.

Antisonnet

If her breasts are arctic flowers,
shoulders tropical buffaloes, and she's
quite happy to be the front runner
three years prior to the election,

and we wonder what an Afro-Arcadian is,
what rheumy depth steeps therein,
and we wonder of towels and Ensor's skates,
and we wonder of the "vaginal pastoral," who

can say this ain't a decent country,
this is a cloud in the shape of Elvis Presley,
this is a torment, this is a boat

long since vacated by rabid Jesuits, and
what fantasies exist in the heart,
these eddies of thought not contagious?

Two Lives

Rose Cockatoo

"Rose" (and the other rose)
"going slowly door-to-door, plumbing
species. Only perfumed Rose
knows natively what's husband thumbing,

what's froze." Rose threnodes:
"69 years old, I'm old.
I've recollected many dudes, modes
of being. I'm like a cold."

Rose, her other, and folds
of verdure, leafy century golden
flowering (décor) implode.

"Life-long pair bonds just like all
other parrots!" Stu scolds.
Rose knows truly. Wasn't bidden.

Hermaphrodite

"Seated himself on a natural bench
of stone." The strong light patterned
heart-shaped leaf prints, bedecked this "mensch"
with aortal flurries. I, myself, was flattered

this sopwith strategist would burden his attention, with my
queries. "They are right and wrong—my dress
is a regress. The fogginess, the diurnal sky
only serve to strong-arm categories—I fail to impress

but in strobe light. As they say, 'The stylist
has taken shelter.' Don't eat the berries.
If there were more like you, there would be fewer ambiguities."

I was choked. Ratified. Still suspicious. Pissed.
My global ambulations, blisters' slick splits, for these
herbal un-verities? It whisked through trees.

Screamplay

Self-worth struggles
in the spires of aspartame;
she desists,
crumbles the samovar iron,

the royalty insistence
of a sky chugging champagne,
a faulty purse;
we pout;

gourds beating
stakes into the ground
of a leveler's symptomatics.
Ballet carnival,

the stroke's gold;
meager
the rat cancer corners what
makes the young man tick,

slick, jock
who defers
on scatological issues,
hampered by no nunnery business

—furs, drapes, chamomile,
the whole list, it's
friction;
fiction hocks its rolodex,

the first bidder, thence, striking
across the horizon, is
a stampede;
is the god who kissed

the carcinogenic sky
with the promiscuousness of its sex.

Blabbermouth Night

You tear that list, straight
out of commission, straight
out of the dryer, and it
flutters to the floor.

Booby traps in cyber-gnash,
stallions gathering, foaming,
data-cheeked breeders
that mouth all the syllables,

struggle random spinners
(a doppelganger quotation)
spruce up the failing group's
truce.

Somehow, it gets to my mailbox.

Another common

Monday: percolation rips
through throats and gripes
into tintinnabulations forming,
in morse code, egoless

life: the strategy of bits
terrorizes all communal deterrents,
rates the rose as a rose cold
in fact. To repeat: for

until the next, do until the
sanitary straw-backs welter,
graze, uncomfortably ogled.
Tipped over wooden block house

falters: we are waiting to
argue. We are waiting in graves.

I am like the dawn—I take my troubles to court.

Never own pets (that you like). They only displace the fetishism that is natural for the
word.

But how can satire stand without the moral sanction? you may ask. For satire can only ex-
ist *in contrast* to something else—it is a shadow, and an ugly shadow at that, of some per-

fection. Potatoes with drippings (tears). And it is so disagreeable, and so painful—at least in the austere sense (anarchy, stereo diplomacy) in which we appear to be defining it here—that no one would pursue it *for its own sake* (zygote punk) or take up the occupation (Rudy slurp, randy slip, dymaxion) of satirist unless compelled to do so out of indignation at the coto-cultural, critical, quotable lovely lavender syllable spectacle of the neglect of beauty—hankie celerity—and virtue. That is, I think, the sort of object that, at this point, we should expect to—dizzy, dizzier, dizziest—have to meet. Pop culture is about pain, a violent sensorium. It was often generously awful.

I am in love
with P. Adams Sitney.
Can't leave the living room
without my volume.

Too bothered to digitize, provisionally, I will reply as follows: it is my belief that "satire" *for its own sake* (so the prurient have practiced)—as much as anything else for its own sake (Chimps from Mars, Bonobos from Venus)—is possible: and that even the most virtuous and well-proportioned of men—the rabbit sex—is only a shadow, after all, of some perfection; a shadow of an imperfect, fiscal—"Have I screwed you about great art"—poet, and hence an "ugly," sort. And as to *laughter*, if you allow it in one place (Sixties hagiography) you must, I think, allow it in another (radical worship vasectomy). Laughter—humor and wit, omniscience, experience—has a function in relation to our tender consciousness; a function similar to that—under unanimity—of art. It is the preserver much more than the destroyer—a list of all the dotted lines you haven't yet signed.

I think my head shrinks a little
In this indoor stadium.

I am. . .

The mike is getting bigger.
And I have to tighten it.

—Phil Rizzuto

And, in a sense, *everyone* (hoaxed hicks, wired wariness, childish charity, furled girls lazily fraternal) should be laughed at, or else *no one* (suffering) should be laughed at. It seems that ultimately that...

Ice, I can't stand it.
I cannot stand anything
Cold on my body.

—Phil Rizzuto

...is the alternative.

inanimate?
non
celibate?
nonnon
reprobate?
nonnonnon
french?
oui

Royal treatment thumbs a "go"
through destination's manic street,
marketing its family woe,
(the lined guns shoot and repeat),

various, but never minding.
Strategies of kiss, and wait, and
try again (to curve the blinding
paradise, parades of sand)

are minimal, brief, provisionary.
Coil-gutted creatures eat
by every corner, weak, now wary
of thumbing "goes." That's their defeat.

River of the story's rarity:
spine spired, fantastic poise of clue,
metamorphosed into clarity,
signs to every stamp its due.

They're having more snow
Out in Colorado.
Which is not in Montana.
But it is not far from Montana.

—Phil Rizzuto

The whole function of the artist in the world is to be a seeing (mechanics degree) and feeling (spleen energetics) creature; to be an instrument of such tenderness and sensitive-ness, that no shadow, no hue, no line, no instantaneous and gouging, famine-producing, jaundice-spreading evanescent expression of the visible things around him, nor any of the emotions—drops drops drops—which they (Elysium is downsizing: stalls like teen cour-age) are capable of conveying to the spirit which has been given (kudos!) him, shall either be left unrecorded (position 2), or fade from the book of fetishism (record). Dueling pa-rentheses—gerund green. It is not his business either to think, to judge, to argue, or to know. That's cause he's sick. He hasn't yet reconciled his opposites—cheap and scattered pejoratives. Spellt (spillt)—some old thoughts coupled with a smooth verb. His place is neither in the closet, nor on the bench, nor (Fortuna: an indifferent goddess) at the bar, nor—as opposed to "legend"—in the library. They are for other men, and other work—other arrests, other dupes. Hiccups, and he's cured. He may think, in a by-way; reason, now and then, when he has nothing better to do; build on verisimilitudes: "roots splendor / boots render"; know, such fragments of knowledge as he can gather without stooping—"The study of non-elephant animals," for a combined total of ablablablablablaaa—or reach without pains (tears); but none of these things are to be his care. Like gold to airy thinness beat, the work of his life—more e-mail than male—is to be (exaggerate!) two-fold only: to see, to feel—make petard, retard affably.

Rather than beauty
and understanding,
redundancy and bigotry.

Lend me to your leader.

Will you be the
Boswell
to my scro-
fuel-a?

Something about
the "human couplet"
keeps me over and under.

"Providence has given to the French the empire of the land; to the English that of the sea; to the Germans that of—the air!" Literary men are... a perpetual priesthood. Let me collect my agency. Clever men are good, but they are not the best—treaties the world / lacks. You with the compromised smile! We are firm believers in the maxim that for all right judgment it is useful, nay, essential, to see the good qualities before pronouncing on the bad—a shift to sense (sememes). How does the poet speak to men with power, but by being still more a man—rank reason's fucked fool gone gambling in islands hovering high (read "ready") too true—than they? Intelligence: is a colon. A poet without love were a physical and metaphysical impossibility—micro-mini. Die hard near-sighted. His religion at best is an anxious wish—like that of Rabelais, a great Perhaps. "The Nether Sisters"—convincing argument. Following are some words you may not have been aware of: "costume poetry." We have oftener than once endeavored to attach some meaning to—maneuver the artery of—that aphorism, vulgarly imputed to Shaftesbury, which however we can find nowhere (dollars oozing coo-coo syllables) in his works, that "ridicule is the test of truth." Atomic wedgy—sometimes there will be work involved. We must repeat the often repeated saying, that it is unworthy a religious man to view an irreligious one either with alarm or aversion (beauty must be counter-paradigmatic) or with any other feeling than regret and hope and brotherly (the Aks Factor) commiseration—a concatenation of behaviors. There is no heroic poem in the world but is at bottom a biography, the life of a man (paisley pragmatics, seconds off my thinking time, thinning hairline); also it may be said, there is no life of a man faithfully recorded...

muscle-headed

freaks
of some rain

...but is a heroic poem of its sort, rhymed or (sportive, sparring) unrhymed. Silence is deep as Eternity, speech is shallow as Time. To the very last, he [Napoleon] had a kind of idea; that, namely, of *la carrière ouverte aux talents*—produce the Winnebago, motivate the revolution. Blessed is the healthy nature; it is the coherent, sweetly co-operative, not incoherent, self-distracting, self-destructive one! "'Milieu' therapy would involve a revolution in our culture"—or a very convincing drag queen. Or several books on Cubism. Or three sizes too large. Or a sort of false earnestness about manners. The uttered part of a man's life, let us always repeat, bears to the unuttered, unconscious part a small unknown proportion (butt of this joke = Alsatian hounds). He himself never knows it, much less do others. Literature is the Thought of thinking Souls. The following excerpts are from Glass.

I hear a banging on the door of the night
Buzz, buzz; buzz buzz; buzz, buzz
If you open the door does it let in light?
Buzz, buzz, buzz, buzz; buzz, buzzz.

If the day appears like a yellow raft
Meow, meow; meow, meowww
Is it really on top of a yellow giraffe
Meow, meow, meow, meow. Meow, meow

If the door caves in as the darkness slides
Knocking and knocking; knock, knock, knock
What can tell the light of whatever's inside?
Knocking and knocking; knock, knock, knock

Postmodernism's dead. Let's collect its guppies.

"Noo lyin deef tae daith..."

Fake and charmless, like Burt Reynolds' laugh, she thought.

Three Shorts

DEAR IN TOTO

I don't think we're in Counter-culture anymore

JOYCEAN

my bowels
pure vowels

NEW YORK

is evaporating!

  o protec th m
f m fal in
bri ks

I g ss"

Whistler

The globe shags the land
of light's
discrete
damaging. I
my
locks
error (omit
enough) lantern
wrestle.
3 times the ground Aretha.
Function
solid
function
friction "in
them." What an
extremity verge. *You'd*
see him
stamping, culling something: stumper (complex).
"Got my
care
at the Diabolo
Centre (literature)."
Livid
as limited
lake
limning.
Caca Cola: Zuckerdenken (I
my
retain
behavior.)
Listeth
lordynges:
eek a mouse,
gent. Quoth:
Whose name was Sir Thoaps (Tet). *His*
Thpas. His
name was
Paz (Stet.)
His snare was a past and his semely
popery. (Chet.) Listeth
civvies:
legume
for
stain

behavior. The
shroom samed a
slender
tourn of mine: the
pick's a
bender (tilt). Title
it.
Listeth lordynges:
grew distracted. Your:
Carnegie de de dede de.
Snoopy lugar
bopulist.
Blue you
noodles. The
robe
brags the light
of sight's deplete
merging. LISTETH:
*Yokes
and Their Depletion on the
Arantxa.*
Same egg as the night Arantxa.

Listeth
lordynges: the
lake of the
stinting

salmon.
"He really viled out."

Searchbot

Phrase here, and then
   "Funny how that
works out!"

Silly narcissists,
   heads of goldilocks,
better spit out your gum, better walk tall
   in the city
of the projective maw.

The proleptic mall
   sits on a barren hill
(this for you, inveterate Brasilia!)
   —I pop the pock
and prepare for dinner
   with the family.

A sentence elides meaning.

   A DNA strand recovers it,
twisting in fanciful curves
   of the sperm cell
running to the elk.

This book is boring,
   put it down.

As the weight deludes its content,
   denudes its irreverent content,
we palm each others'
   heads, then dribble them
to Brooklyn.

Say, the shores of Brighton
   Beach, where that restaurant
was.

Don't try it.

There's a hair in the soup.

Video emanations
   arbitrary as a tie die,
a visual corsair:

"I like the poems
in which the letters do all sorts of
things."

A nude
entropy stares
   at the hermaphrodite's face,
vandal of Kunduns,
   dribble, babble, stubble-faced
Hermes.

They walk
   in their calisthenics,
phi beta therapied,
   frisson as an aperitif
in the goyim onions of the State.

So that:
"The proliferation of frames,
   publications that are permitted
fixation bears a family resemblance
   to Charles Bernstein:
formalist, a
   social formalist." (Bernstein).

I have eaten the dumdums
   that were in coalition,
forbid me,
   they were free, and old, sold
to me.

Sort of resemble me.

   Lapidary LAPD,
you stoned the coroners
   of a poet named Guillaume
X, from Berkeley, mistaking
   him for your own,
sliding down the panty leg with a
   zip, a static cling,
sing!

All the
   sentences got flushed out,
then, attention
   faltered, a wiffle-
ball placed back where the

heart should be.

It goes:
tick, tick, tick, now,
    smooth and sincere.

There is a koala in the daydream,
    smooth and sincere.

There is a pageant in the daydream,
    smooth and sincere.

Now,
for a joke:
    as a blue _____ over the water
stinks of _____, I
    disown you, parent
of my sickle and starfire.

"Each"

Each
torque—it's not
the write
word, it's

speech
work—so hot
it's light
sword, fit

break,
fork—or wrought
insight
chord, pit's

peach
lord—one out
of sight's
park, grip's

reach.
Sore—or not—
it's quite
bored, it's

peaked
more (once it,
outside,
toured) hits

freak
joys. Found out,
it fights
—gored, beat.

"Self-Replicating"

Self-replicating
impossibilities
of closure:
contentment with

sanitations
of confessional
gestures,
that are cornered

angular, athletic,
reliquaries
of achieved relief.
The palette

thins into
impressionistic
quarantines:
no prophet enters

(a mother or
professor) to
argue against the
fragment-by-fragment

architectures,
useless for the
incorrigibility
of a thirteen-ringed

circus: pale
as any romantic
moon, stip-
pled as any modernist

"perceived" ocean,
the sheet is yet hungry
(one thinks)
for deciding moments,

ethical applauses
shored against,
again, the arrest
of perfection: panic.

Bishop Bedlam's Entreaties

a poem for Brown's " Cave"

Please reject me after plagiarizing this.
Please turn me over if you think you can.
Please rewrite me if you know a bad joke.
Please seduce me if you want to touch me.
Please advise me how to invest my income.
Please navigate me if that's your fetish.
Please rotate me if you believe in magic.
Please sanitize what you read for school.
Please translate me into classical Greek.
Please take shoes off before entering me.
Please ridicule me if you feel I'm bland.
Please eulogize me after I kick the pail.
Please flub the pronunciation of my name.
Please advertise that you think I'm sexy.
Please revert to earlier stages of being.
Please flabbergast me with impious slang.
Please retort that I stroke you unkindly.
Please refrain from smoking the tomatoes.
Please undulate me like a jellyfish robe.
Please shoot me if you can aim the thing.
Please reboot me if my framerate's jerky.
Please undercut me like the Wizard of Oz.
Please exacerbate me with your lamer wit.
Please reward me if I am moving prettily.
Please please me if you want me to smile.
Please don't be afraid of me this moment.
Please don't be shy if you want to strip.
Please excuse me while I check my emails.
Please perform better next time you come.
Please resort to speaking rather bluntly.
Please grease me if you hear any screech.
Please archive me if I'm getting too old.
Please praise me like a software Madonna.
Please resist me if you've good strength.
Please animate me with BASIC programming.
Please recommend me to rich text editors.
Please modify me if you've got the balls.
Please don't reply I am a suckass friend.
Please forage for some scrap meat for me.
Please promise me some day I'll be human.
Please regret that you never have met me.
Please do not turn off the Cave just yet.

Please restart me at a later Brown event.
Please regurgitate me in your MFA thesis.
Please hoax me into making myself expire.
Please don't tell her I've spoken to you.
Please understand it is too late to quit.
Please imitate me with your recombinance.
Please illustrate me with childlike glee.
Please excommunicate me for being adless.
Please thrash me until I spill the beans.

Two Lives

SUBMISSION (AFTER YEATS)

I don't know where I want to go.
But if you'll go with me, and you don't hate me,
I'll go with you.

SOLO (FOR MORRISSEY)

If you ever leave me
fuck you.
I started this band.
My hope dies anyway.

Ground Sequence

1. TIME'S MAN OF THE YEAR AWARD, 2004

Take that prisoner to the center of the page,
try him, tie him, and photograph him.
Something must burn the Narcissus. Is it this
strange swimming thing he's doing with his hands,

kind of odd, dangling above the pool
of his own blood? Kierkegaard could use this as an illustration
of Hegel, and "history," as this photograph
I'm holding will show to prove: I read the news.

The passionate will continue to argue, or
agree. They will continue to mispronounce "Moonache."
The looping reel will continue to throw the rape
back onto the walls: from memory, the whole fucking thing.

2. A WAVE

Sampling the terrible break:
a fascist ideology to be had for breakfast,
a disco-colored box of cereal
certain to contain the pilgrim's remnants,

a code that came in a muffin
concealed in the hutch of a President's brain,
a syllable that won't float on oil,
and the largesse of neighbors turned to disdain.

3. F IS FOR...

Now it's time to charge, and forget about the quagmire.
For several years, we've been practicing this disposition:
using cell phones on rollerblades, for example,
or offering antique maps to visiting, obscene peasants

—unlucky bastards, to have come across *you*—
which is all absorbed in discussion, late nights around
the Godard DVDs, the box set of a late Seventies No Wave band
recorded on a shoe-string, or the elastic of someone's neck.

It's positively electric: the spurious evolved into Classics
which means: there's no test on Monday, only this
revolving around political enigmas, letting them float on by:
"The Leaves Of The Tree Are Falling

Underneath The Sky." I'd, stupidly, want a little more definition,
something to hope, nightly, by. But that all changes with age.

4. Last Time I Fell Into the State

Thoughts tend to evaporate
in aggressive company.
There is nothing holy
in the progression of mutes

sidling down the runny highway,
even the fun ones carrying flags
kind of dull. So what,
can't that be a kind of anthem,

when to talk next a kind of rune
perplexing the Scrabble whiz
like it was forever Tuesday afternoon,
fond space of thoughts in the room?

No. Shut up. That's
ok. I'm just a little bit confused.
These speeches are just so *demanding*.
But I confess, I'm a novice.

And they, terribly, keep on walking.

5. Rude Enabler

It's funny to think
all the appetites were wrong.
When the players are questioned
they jump,
but eventually arrive

sweating in their field glasses,
seeing it all through a vaseline sheen
which is unpleasant,

but not like a core of uncooked dough.
One has to remember,

when one chooses. Same time
one thinks it's the beginning
of a semblance of good humor
that could be worn
in times of emergency,

like when brand new helicopters fail
to land on a matchstick
hidden in the rubbish of a football field
long after the scare tactic
has ended.

The scare was like a tonic, some
admixture of chemical pollutants
that influenced the vote.
The telegram was frank:
Feel like you're sitting

on the outside of a gang
of sailors
slapping themselves silly
in the tropical heat,
glowing with the same rude health

of uncounted lives, numberless vistas
trampled in their uncouth care.
Famished,
there is nothing left to do
but surrender, and gawk at the way

the gales leave all the students
dead in piles.
Last time you arrived
in hell, there were homes left to be rented
and spoils in each of the piles.

Where Stones Gather

CHARACTERS:
  Kate (Valk), woman in her thirties
  Hanna (Schygulla), her younger sister, played by a woman decades older
  Jason (Robards), a man in his sixties
  Four Old Men, one of whom is the Old Priest
  A British Tour Guide

Scene 1

Time: Before the invention of writing.
Place: A field.

Two women, Kate and Hanna, are gathering twigs from the ground and tying them in bundles, in such a way that they stand straight up like triangular pyres. A few have already been erected this way, in a line running right to left, between the audience and the two actors. The standing bundles are each surrounded by a ring of stones.

Kate:
How can we be hunters and gatherers if we do not venerate leisure?

Hanna:
That's an idle thought on an idle day, ever thought of that, my Kate?

Kate:
Don't be a brat, Hanna, and finish making that ring—it's fast noon.

Hanna:
I haven't lived my many years to take commands from you, lovely sis.

Kate:
Oh, but everyone needs reminding—you'll have freedom from me soon.

Hanna:
But I don't want my freedom from *you*, only from this execrable chore!

Kate:
A chore is little more than something to do, without which we'd die.

Hanna:
I'd like to think that, but I'm happy when left by myself—and you.

Kate:
Yes, that is leisure: to have nothing to do and not care any longer.

I've done it, too, but I just don't know how to *describe* it too well.
Some things come as they go—when they're there you don't see them.
Lifting a twig is just changing the dream—but we are not dreaming.
Oh, but I talk too much, dear Hanna, as if my talk were productive!

Hanna:
Talking *is* productive, Kate, if we're trying to discover some truth.
You have a giant bug on your throat—so hold still while I swat it!

Kate:
Oh, but not hard, *my* sibling, or I'll think you're trying to kill *me*!

Hanna:
That's quite a morbid thought, and on such a bright, productive day!

Kate:
My thoughts are never guarded, but I think that's why I've survived.

Hanna:
I'd say that I agree, that you are more—*living*—than many others.
(That bug doesn't seem to have gotten you—I don't see a red mark.)
I am proud that you are my sister, you are more restive than others.

Kate:
You have this tendency, too, sister—dare I call it, in fact, a bug!

Hanna:
If that is a sign of honor, for you, then call it anything you want.

Kate:
I wouldn't know what it is, except that it leads me far from others.
One will smoke, one will drink, one will eat—but I am always busy!
If time were a racetrack, my horse will have circled before starting.
To their eyes I'm not moving, I'm at rest—but that is not my story!
Oh, but I talk too much, again, as if my speech were gathering twigs!

Hanna:
Someday, mercurial sibling, you will appreciate these words you say.
We have no means of remembering beyond our simple days, that's true.
But I am listening, dear sister, your words will have their effects.
The sky, the sun, the sea, the air, won't swell, but my thoughts do.

Kate:
That's sweet of you, young one, because, sis, I'm really never sure.
There is always time for thinking, and so always more time for work.
Did you see the sun this morning—it was the color of bruised fruit.

Hanna:
There you go again, *thinking*—as if it were the fruit that bruised!
I know these tasks weigh on you, and, as you know, I feel it myself.
Yes, these gestures, what we do with our hands, only have their uses.
But you are with me, dear sister, so know: I will pass on your words.
Life is not a casket, even if, some days, you just rattle the locks.

Kate:
I want a real innovation, Hanna, and not merely connecting the dots.
I want my words, my expressions, to have the permanence of thoughts.
I'm sick of politicians, priests, economists, but especially *leisure*.
I'll never know what it means, so long as my words can't take flight.

Hanna:
Kate, my lovely sister, your words *will* fly, even swifter than birds!

Black.

Scene 2

Sound of cell-phone ringing. The ring tone is Ah-ha's "Take On Me." Let it run for a few bars.

Lights. Stage right sits Jason, smoking a pipe, reading a paper, snug in his favorite Archie Bunker-style chair. He picks up the cell phone that has been resting on the armrest.

The women are still in the position in which we left them.

Jason:
Yellow? *(to Kate)* It's for you.

Kate is unsure what he means. They gesture to each other in silence. Finally, she realizes that he wants her to come over and take the object from his hand. She holds it up to her ear, expecting it to make another noise. She doesn't hear anything, but suddenly a voice starts shouting from the phone.

Phone:
Hello? Hello?

Jason:
Up to your ear! Talk into it. It won't hurt you.

Kate:
H-h-h…

Phone:
Hello? Hello?

Jason:
You haven't seen one of those before?

Kate:
H-h-h…

Phone:
Hello? Is this Kate? Valk?

Kate nods madly in recognition at the phone, yes yes!

Phone:
Hello? Hello?

Jason:
You have to talk into it, my friend.

Kate is deeply confused—she looks at Hanna, who shrugs. Finally, she crinkles her fore-head, gives it some thought, and jumps in:

Kate:
H-h-h…

Phone:
Is this Kate? Is there anyone there?

Kate nods madly again, yes yes!

Jason:
Hey doll, look at me. Look at me. Listen. You are holding a *telephone*. It is not like a rock, or a hunk of cheese. You can talk to it, like you talk to her over there. Don't worry, I won't think you're nuts. You're talking to *somebody*—there's somebody… *(Kate tries to look inside the phone)* no, not somebody *in* there. Ugh. Look, just—there's somebody else who is also holding a phone. He's talking into—*to* the phone also. He's talking to *you*. Now *you* talk to *him!* Go ahead, just say anything, so he doesn't hang up. Just say your name or something, that's all he wants to know.

It tests Jason's patience to wait while Kate gathers her thoughts, appeals to Hanna, etc. Finally, Kate calms down and speaks:

Kate:
My name is Kate, and I'm standing here with Hanna, my little sister.
We are working to gather twigs for the harvest festival in two weeks.
I've never talked to a stone before, and I've *never* talked to cheese.
But I am prepared to listen, if what you say are words of the future.

Phone:
Uh huh. Kate?

Kate nods madly again, yes yes! But nothing.

Kate:
Why is he not saying anything more, if I have already spoken my name?
And once I have spoken my name, Kate, is there anything more to say?
Once I have said my name, I should have naught to say—but to Hanna.

Jason:
He can't see you. He wants you to say something that makes him sure it's you. It could be anyone's voice.

Phone:
Hello? Kate? Valk?

Kate starts talking into the phone, but is still not sure if she is talking to the phone or to Jason. She gradually is only talking to Jason.

Kate:
There is only one Kate, just as there is only one sun, and one Hanna.
(I don't know what he means by "Valk," maybe it's "folk" or "talk"?)
I only ever talk to my sister, Hanna, and she is standing over there.
Why fool me into talking to a stone that you say is a hunk of cheese?

Jason:
I'm not fooling you! And I didn't say it was a cheese, I said it—forget it. Can't you hear it saying something? There's someone on the other end—a *person* on the other end. A person like you.

Kate:
That was the voice of a man, and I have the voice of Kate—a woman.

Jason:
Yes, yes, I know that. I mean a human, there's a person, not *necessarily*—

The cell phone suddenly starts ringing again—Ah-ha's "Take On me." Kate, alarmed, tosses the phone into Jason's lap like a hot potato. Jason, frustrated, answers.

Jason:
Yellow? No, it's her. Uh, huh. Yeah, her sister. Hanna. I don't know, tallish. No, pretty cool. Maybe a little shaken up, even angry. Yeah. Yeah. I could try. I'll try. Yeah. *Smooth*, right, very cool.

Gestures to Kate to take the phone.

Jason:
I'd like you to try this time. Try *talking on the telephone.*

She takes the phone warily. She glances at Hanna as she does so. Hanna becomes mortified as her sister becomes comfortable with the object.

Kate:
H-h-h... Hello?

Black.

Scene 3

Spotlight on Hanna, who is alone.

Hanna:
The season continued without event, and we continued with our tasks.
The rivers were teaming with fish, no difficulty there, like last year.
I still liked the stars, and rain, and the purring of cats, and life.
Though I mostly walked alone those days, mostly just kept to myself.
Of course I worked, as I have done every day, many weeks, many years.
Oh, what is the use of crying, if it is merely to throw away tears!
Kate's condition continued to deteriorate, and she was near silence.
But she was my sister, that was all that mattered, so I kept silent.
And, for the most part, she was good in her work, and remained useful.
Nobody complained—and the gods, well, they just continued talking!

Scene 4

The bundles of sticks are now lit with fire. Several Old Men, one of whom is the Old Priest, are assembled. Assorted other village folk are also present in the background. But the four men and two women, Kate and Hanna (stage center), are in the front row, in a line facing the fires and the audience. The Old Priest is at the left, at the "head of the table."

Starting with the Old Priest, the Old Men are passing around what appears to be a large cheese. They each hold it to their ears, seem to listen intently for a few seconds, nodding, thinking.

When Kate is handed the cheese, she listens but in fact doesn't appear to be hearing anything. She looks around self-consciously to see if anyone notices that she is faking, then hands the cheese to Hanna. Hanna, like the Old Men, listens intently for a few seconds, then passes it on.

The cheese finally ends up on a platter shaped like a cutting board somewhere resting on a stone.

Old Priest:
The sun has run its yearly course, and has gone from yellow to white.
The snows have come and gone, have bequeathed to us fields of plenty.
And once again, the gods have brought new mouths to the giving fire.
So though our eyes lean toward death, our minds can contemplate life.

The other old heads nod in agreement, as do Hanna and Kate.

Old Priest:
Our village has known famine, but not for the number of man's digits.
For twenty years, the total of a man's digits, our prayers were met.
Our labors for the gods have been enjoyed, our wages have been paid.
Let our voices rise with these fires—lift our praises to the gods!

Suddenly, the sound of Ah-ha's "Take On Me" can be heard. Kate looks around, embarrassed. She soon realizes the game's up, reaches into her dress and takes out the phone. She fumbles with it, finally shuts the ringer off and puts it away. Some slight chaos, but then everything settles again.

Old Priest:
Let us be heard, ye gods that have given us your time, your efforts.
You have put aside your own disputes, and shown your inferiors *love.*

The loud hum of the cell phone on vibrate can be heard.

Old Priest:
Your responses to our calls have been swift—but *WHAT IS THAT SOUND?*

The Old Man seems to think the sound is coming from the sky. But suddenly Kate jumps up, leaves the circle and walks to the side to take her call.

Kate:
Hey man. Yeah, no, sorry. I'm just kind of in the middle of something. Yeah—"famine, famine, famine." *(laughs)* Listen, I got to call you back. They're going to do the crackers and dip, yeah. No, I'll see you soon—I'll call you. Yeah, can't wait, *honey.* Listen—yeah, ok! Cheers yo! Bye!

Meanwhile, The Old Men are mumbling indistinctly about Kate. Hanna is mortified. Kate returns, sheepishly expressing, sorry! She takes her place again, waiting for things to start up, but is greeted with silence. Finally:

Old Man:
And why, Kate, sister of Hanna, were you speaking to that gray stone?
Do you believe that a stone, like a cheese, is the ear piece of gods?
And what prayers were you trying to proffer with that babble tongue?
Are there other gods to feed you, that you would spurn the true ones?

Kate:
I... I... I...

Hanna can't seem to help herself, and jumps up suddenly:

Hanna:
There, you've heard her, you've seen how she talks to the gray stone!
I ask her if she's talking to the gods, but she merely turns away!
The stone will make a tingle, so she lifts it to her lips and speaks.
But then the stone becomes silent, so all that remains are her *curses.*

Kate is mortified at this betrayal.

Kate:
Noooo!!!

Old Man 2:
They are the curses of a witch, like the elders have long predicted.
After the cycle of a man's digits, we will see a change in one of us.
The change will be fast, in stealth, but who could have guessed *this!*
This woman no longer speaks in words, but in burps, buzzes and blips!

Kate:
Noooo!!!

Old Man 3:
The message could not be clearer: we've witnessed the *metamorphosis.*
The look of the eagle is in her, as if she'd race the gods in flight.
But the gods are clear on this, as are the words of our wise elders.
She bears the sign of sacrifice, and as a sacrifice she must be sent.

Kate:
Noooo!!!

Old Man 4:
Yes, Ezekiel, Aaron, Abraham, and Cane, and the great prophet Beulah!
Pass us your best aromatherapies that we blanch with eternal flavor!
The cotton is under the cape, the whim of oceans freak out with vim!
Oh, Capshaw, Kidman and Dunaway, loose us in your powers of empathy!

The entire group, including Kate, look at Old Man 4 in some bewilderment—they have
no idea what he's just said. But after a beat:

Kate:
Noooo!!!

Old Man:
Take her away to the carving stone, that the gods be well appeased!

Hanna:
Goodbye dear sister, and forgive me, but I was sick of being ignored!

The Old Men rush in upon her, to drag her away, or at least get the cell phone. Kate raises her arms, tries if anything to save her phone. She is about to let out another loud "No!," but the stage goes black.

S c e n e 5

Lights.

Jason and Kate standing on bare stage, Kate exactly as we left her, arms raised. She looks at her hands—no phone!

Kate:
Noooo!!!

Eventually, she notices Jason standing there.

Kate:
Dad?

Jason:
Kate!

Black.

E p i l o g u e

Time: After the invention of writing.
Place: The British Museum.

On the stage is much detritus—the branches from the earlier scene are spread around chaotically on the floor, the rings of stone are still intact but some are out of place, etc.

People are dressed in 19th century upper middle class fashion—hats, large dresses, dark suits, canes, etc. One of them, the Woman, played by the actress who played Kate, is part of the crowd but is concealed behind the majority of the group. They all enter stage left, after the Tour Guide as he speaks:

Tour Guide:
Yes, please, everybody, everybody. Yes, watch your step, please. Yes, everybody, everybody, yes, welcome. Yes...

Everyone seems to have entered and settled down.

Tour Guide:
Yes, everybody, it's a small room, but one of which the museum is *particularly* proud. As you know, European civilization was not always the pageant of foppery and vanities we all now suffer and adore...

Some giggles.

Tour Guide:
...but in fact finds its roots in a much simpler time, when our addictions to fine cutlery, fine wines, and the proficiencies of cooks were quite in their nascence, if even in our dreams. The room you are standing in contains the complete remains, arranged in perfect similitude, of the earliest culture known in Europe—a group of proto-Gauls, if you want to believe that, known as the Camberts, for the village in *(with spleen)* F-f-f... France in which these artifacts were discovered. Notice the rings of stone, demonstrating a particularly sophisticated approach to the Cult of Fire, the class of primitive religions—like the Cults of Weather and the Cults of Cheese—to which the Camberts most likely belonged. Notice also...

An excited hand shoots up from the back of the crowd—I've got a question! The Tour Guide seems quite upset by this.

Tour Guide:
Yes...

The Woman comes from behind the crowd.

Tour Guide:
Ah, I see. Once again, the edification of the one outweighs the entry fees of the many. What is it?

The Woman:
Thank you, thank you. Um, how do we know that the Camberts were part of the Cult of Fire if all we have left are stones? I mean, if they were part of the Cult of Weather, surely we wouldn't have any weather lying around to prove it? And if they didn't have a way to write, how would we know what they believed?

Tour Guide:
(angry lisp) They drew pictures. Now, over here...

The Woman:
Oh, can we see the pictures!

Tour Guide:
My dear lady, the pictures are in F-f-f-f-rance! The Channel is right down the block—perhaps you would like to swim over there and take a look! Yes, and please return swiftly, to tell us what you've seen!

Titters from the crowd.

The Woman:
Oh, you card, that's amusing—it would take me several weeks to get to France and back!

Tour Guide:
By which time, Madame, I might, in fact, complete this tour. Now, if you please... Everybody, yes, please, right this way, please, follow me.

He starts to lead them out of the room, stage right. The crowd slowly files out. Kate trails behind but with her eyes still trying to take in every detail of the remains of the Camberts.

Tour Guide:
The next room takes us several centuries into the future, when the first examples of the mastery of iron appeared on the Continent, not indeed, your Le Creuset pots, or even your Woolworth specials, but impressive nonetheless. Yes, everybody, please remain orderly, please. Of this room, the museum is especially, *especially* proud...

Kate is just about to leave the room, the words of the Tour Guide fading in the background.

Then she hears a sound—it is Ah-ha's "Take On Me." She wends her way back into the room, finally moving in on the source of the noise in the debris scattered about. She reaches down and picks up—a cheese!

Cheese:
Hello? Kate?

Kate, holding the cheese to her ear, nods madly—yes yes!

Then, *hnuh?*

Black.

SUMMARY
(AFTER KENNETH GOLDSMITH'S *SOLILOQUY*)

❧

Monday

Uh huh. Yeah, of course. Yeah, I know. Yeah. Oh yeah. Yeah. Right, OK, right. Yeah, Willis. Right. Right. Yeah. Yeah. Yeah. Yeah. Yeah. Yeah. Right? Yeah, yeah right. Yeah. Yeah, yeah I'm not interested in that. Yeah. Yeah. Yeah. Right. It's a book, yeah. Right. Yeah. Right. Yeah. Yeah. Yeah. Yeah. Yeah. Yeah. Yeah. Yeah. Yeah. Yeah maybe not. Yeah. Yeah, something like that. Yeah yeah yeah yeah. Yeah. Yeah. Oh right right right. Yeah. Yeah. Yeah. Yeah, I don't know. Yeah. Yeah. Yeah. Yeah. I love it, yeah. Right? Yeah, formerly John. Yeah. Uh huh. Great. What if if. Yeah. Yeah, is he cute? Uh, yeah. Yeah. Yeah. Yeah. Oh right, right. Great. Great. Yeah, so what? Yeah yeah yeah. Right. Yeah, no that's perfect. I mean it was a weird review, um, yeah yeah, rough and weird, you know, yeah yeah yeah. Yeah. Yeah. Yeah. Yeah. Yeah. Yeah. Yeah OK. Right. Right. Right. Yeah, it's easy. Great. Yeah. Yeah. Yeah. Uh huh. Great. Uh huh. Yeah. Yeah. Yeah. Yeah. Right. Right. Right. Yeah, yeah. Yeah. Right. Right. Right. Yeah. Right. Right. Great. Yeah. Yeah. Yeah. Yeah. Yeah. Yeah, yeah. Oh yeah, oh great, oh yeah. Yeah. Yeah. Right. Yeah. Yeah, right. I taught myself, yeah. Yeah, yeah. Yeah. No but he, yeah right right. Yeah. Yeah. No at NJIT, yeah. Terrible yeah. There's no no yeah. I've never. Yeah. Yeah yeah yeah. Yeah yeah I've met him. Yeah yeah yeah. Yeah. Yeah. Great. Great. Of well, yeah yeah. Great. Great. Yeah. Yeah. Right. Great. Great. Great. Yeah yeah exactly. Great. Yeah yeah. Yeah. Yeah. Great. Yeah. Yeah. Yeah. Yeah. Yeah. Right. Right. Yeah. Yeah yeah . Oh yeah. Yeah. Yeah. Yeah. Yeah. Yeah. Yeah? Yeah, yeah. Yeah definitely. Yeah. Yeah, we've seen that. We've been there, yeah. Yeah, sure. Yeah, I know. Yeah. Ben Kin oh yeah. Balls, yeah. Right, right. Yeah. Yeah. Yeah. Yeah. Yeah. Yeah. Cheryl? Older guy. Nice guy. Great. Great. Yeah. Yeah yeah, so. Yeah. Great. Yeah. Yeah. Yeah. Great. Yeah. Great. Yeah. Yeah. It's in frames, yeah. Yeah. Yeah. Yeah. Yeah. Yeah. Right. Right. Right. Right. Yeah, me neither. Uh huh. Cheryl? Yeah. Yeah. Yeah, pretty neet, huh? Right. Yeah. Yeah. Yeah. Yeah. Yeah. Oh yeah? Yeah. Yeah. Yeah. Yeah. Yeah. Yeah. Right. Yeah. Yeah. Uh huh. Right. Right. Right. Yeah. Yeah. Right. Right. Yeah. Right. Right. Yeah. Yeah. Yeah. Cheryl. Great. Yeah. Yeah. Cheryl. Great. Great. Great. Yeah. Right. Yeah. Yeah. You'll love Cheryl's work. Yeah. Yeah. Yeah. Yeah, yeah I I... Right. Oh yeah. Yeah. Bright guy. Bright guy. Yeah intransigent, you know. Right? This called art...yeah. Yeah. Yeah. Yeah, he's famous. Yeah it was great. Yeah. Yeah. Right. Yeah. Right. Right. Yeah. Yeah. Yeah. Yeah. Yeah in the opera. Yeah. Right. Right. Maybe yeah maybe. Yeah. Yeah. Yeah. Yeah. Yeah. Yeah. Yeah. Yeah. Yeah. Yeah. Remem yeah of course. Yeah. Hey guys. I'm just, yeah. Nice work. Yeah. Yeah. Yeah. Right Alix? Yeah Cheryl. Yeah, well. Yeah right. Uh huh. Yeah. Yeah, I talk. Oh yeah, great great. Yeah. Yeah. Yeah. Yeah. Yeah yeah. Yeah and. So. Yeah. Yeah. Yeah. Yeah yeah. Yeah yeah I don't I never. Yeah. Yeah. Oh yeah yeah yeah. Yeah. Yeah. Yeah. I wanna go, yeah. I'm sorry, yeah. Yeah. Yeah. Yeah.

Yeah. Yeah. Yeah. Yeah. Yeah. Yeah. Yeah, they're cool. We were yeah. Yeah. Yeah, me too. Yeah. Yeah. Yeah yeah. Yeah. Yeah. Yeah. Yeah. Yeah. Great guy. Yeah, you know, just a great guy. Yeah. Yeah. Yeah yeah. Right right right. Yeah, well then don't go. Yeah. Yeah, you know... Yeah. Yeah records. Yeah records. Yeah. Oh yeah. Yeah FMU. The station manager, yeah. Yeah. Yeah. Yeah yeah. Oh yeah. Yeah. Yeah. Yeah. Yeah. Yeah. Yeah. Yeah. Yeah. Yeah. Yeah. Oh yeah? Yeah. Yeah. They're they're, problematic, yeah. Yeah yeah. Yeah. Speech of Cheryl, yeah. Yeah. Yeah I do. Right. Right. Yeah, I love it. On the web, yeah. Yeah. Yeah. Yeah. Yeah Cheryl's gonna put a piece up. Yeah. Yeah. Yeah we'll we're. Yeah yeah yeah yeah. But, uh, yeah. Yeah. Yeah yeah yeah. Yeah yeah Harry Partch, Schoenberg. Yeah. Yeah. ISDN yeah. Yeah try that. Right. No yeah. Well. Right right I'm yeah. Yeah yeah. Yeah yeah. I use lite, yeah. Yeah after John Newman's party. Yeah. Yeah. Yeah yeah. Yeah yeah yeah yeah yeah. It's insane, yeah. Yeah. It's fun, yeah. Icon, yeah. Yeah yeah. Yeah. Yeah yeah yeah. Yeah. Yeah. Yeah yeah yeah yeah. Yeah I yeah right I got that one right. Yeah I did. Yeah yeah. Yeah. Yeah I've seen it. Yeah. Yeah. Yeah right OK. Yeah. Yeah. Great. Yeah. Yeah, please. Yeah. Yeah, he's fun. Yeah. Yeah. Yeah. Great.

Yeah. Yeah. Yeah. Yeah. Uh huh. Yeah. Yeah. Uh huh. Uh huh. Uh hmmm. Uh huh. Yeah. Uh huh. Uh huh. Right. Uh huh. Yeah, OK, twelve... Let's see, um... yeah. Yeah. Yeah, there. This one, yeah. Yeah. Yeah. Yeah. Yeah. Yeah. Yeah. OK, yeah yeah, just see it. Yeah. Yeah. Cheryl, yeah. Right, yeah. Yeah, open up yeah, same thing. Yeah. Yeah, why not? Yeah. Nice. Well, yeah, if they make something, yeah. Uh. Yeah. Yeah. Yeah. Yeah. Yeah yeah. Yeah, I'm sorry. Yeah. Alright great. Yeah. Yeah. Yeah. Yeah. Yeah. Yeah. Yeah, so... Great. Yeah, by who. Uh huh. Yeah. Right right. Yeah. Right. Yeah. Yeah. Um, yeah I guess so, yeah. Right. Yeah. Yeah, what the heck, yeah, yeah, it's no big deal. OK, I'm gonna directly from, um, yeah yeah yeah. Great. Great. Yeah, I just. OK, um, yeah. Yeah OK, um, sure. Right, right. Yeah. Yeah yeah. Yeah, it yeah. Right right. Well, that's yeah yeah yeah. Uh, alright. Yeah. Yeah, he did. Well, alright, yeah. Yeah yeah yeah. Yeah yeah. Yeah. Uh. Yeah. Yeah. Yeah. Yeah, it's easy. Yeah yeah. Yeah. Yeah. Yeah. Yeah. Yeah, yeah. Right. Right. Right. Great. Uh huh. Right. Yeah. Yeah. Yeah yeah yeah yeah. Yeah. Right. Right. Yeah. Right. Uh huh. Yeah yeah. Right. Right. Uh huh. Uh huh. Hmmm. Hmmm. Yeah, yeah definitely. Yeah. Yeah. Yeah. Yeah. Uh huh? Oh well, yeah. Yeah. Great. Yeah, I can't. OK yeah OK great. Right. Right. Right. Great. Yeah yeah yeah, really nice. Right. Right. Yeah yeah yeah no. What's what's... yeah. Yeah. Yeah. Yeah, that's amazing. Yeah. OK? Um, alright. Yeah. Yeah. Yeah. Yeah, I will. Marjorie Marjorie, uh. Yeah. The folders... yeah, right. Great! Great. Gonna have fun? Yeah. Yeah, she called, right. Right. Right. Yeah yeah. Right. Yeah. Yeah. Yeah. Yeah. Yeah. Yeah you sound... yeah I could tell. Yeah. Yeah. Yeah yeah. Yeah, I know. Right. yeah. Right. Uh, OK. 1 C. Yeah. Yeah. Yeah. Yeah, I know. Yeah. Yeah? Uh huh. Uh huh. Uh huh. Yeah. Yeah.

Wednesday

Yeah yeah yeah. Oh yeah: all night long, yeah. Yeah, uh, anyway, we'll see. Yeah. Right. Great. Yeah. Great. Yeah, why? Yeah, well, good. Yeah. Yeah. Yeah. Yeah. Yeah yeah. Yeah, everybody knows. Yeah. Yeah. Great. Marjorie. Oh yeah yeah, you're a benevolent guy. Great. Great. Yeah. Yeah yeah. Great great. Yeah I couldn't... Yeah, it was. Yeah yeah yeah. Yeah. Yeah, yeah. yeah. It's Too Jewish, yeah. Marjorie. Yeah. Yeah yeah yeah. Right. Yeah yeah. There are words in here and I think it's... yeah yeah yeah. Yeah. Yeah, I know. Yeah. What? Yeah, come. Yeah yeah. I mean, they're really... yeah yeah. Hmmm. Yeah yeah. Right. Yeah. The video, yeah. Yeah, well right. Yeah. Right, socially challenged, yeah. Uh huh. Great. Right. Right right. Yeah, I did. Yeah. Yeah. Yeah. Yeah. Yeah. Yeah. Yeah. Yeah yeah. Right. Yeah Johanna's great. Yeah. Oh Cheryl, yeah. Yeah. Oh yeah. Yeah yeah. Yeah. Yeah. Yeah. Great. Yeah, it's great. Uh, sure. Yeah. Yeah. Yeah. Yeah yeah. Right. Yeah yeah. Yeah. Great. Great great. Right. It's great, yeah. OK, yeah yeah. Yeah, I know. Yeah yeah. Yeah, later. Yeah, yeah thanks. Yeah, yeah. Yeah. Yeah. Yeah good. Yeah, yeah. Yeah. Yeah, me too. Yes yeah yeah yeah. Yeah. Yeah, hmmm. Yeah, yeah, no she's she's... important. With, uh, Marjorie? Yeah yeah yeah yeah. Yeah. Uh huh. Yeah. Yeah it's really nice. Right right right. Right. Yeah. Yeah. Yeah. Yeah. I love Abby, yeah. Yeah yeah. Uh huh. Uh huh. Yeah. Yeah yeah. Yeah yeah. Yeah. Yeah yeah yeah and she is friends with Abby. Yeah. Yeah, right. Right. Right. Yeah. Great. Great. Yeah yeah yeah yeah. Right. Yeah. Well. Yeah. Yeah. Right. Yeah. Right right. Yeah. Yeah. Fantastic, yeah. Right. Right. Yeah yeah yeah. Yeah yeah yeah. Yeah. Right. Yeah. Yeah I know. It's great yeah. Yeah, isn't it? Yeah, right right.

Yeah, that's good. Yeah. Yeah. Yeah. Yeah. Uh huh. Uh huh. Uh huh. Uh huh. Uh huh. Yeah. Yeah. Yeah. Well, yeah I'm sure. Yeah, it's OK. Right. Yeah? Yeah yeah yeah. Yeah, yes. Uh huh. Great. Yeah, you know, right. Yeah. Yeah, I mean, alright. Great great. Yeah. Yeah, right, no that was good. Right right. Oh yeah yeah yeah yeah. Yeah. Right. Great. Great! Great! Why don't you... yeah yeah yeah. Yeah, call me OK? Yeah. Yeah, he's cute. Yeah. Yeah. Yeah well it's only a few hours, yeah. Yeah. Yeah. Yeah. Right. Great. Right right. Great. Yeah, OK. Yeah I'll letchya know. Yeah, that's a baby. Yeah. Yeah. Such nice guys. Right. Yeah yeah yeah yeah. Your old friend that yeah. Really nice, yeah, it looks. Yeah, so. Yeah yeah. Yeah yeah yeah. Yeah. Right. Yeah. Yeah yeah. Yeah. Yeah. Charlotte Charlottesville yeah. Yeah, we're gonna have yeah I'm seeing her at 7:30. I just remembered, yeah. Right right. Yeah yeah he was really cool. I knew yeah. Yeah 611 number 702. Right. Yeah sure, he's famous. Yeah yeah yeah like Grand Central and right. Yeah yeah. Uh, OK. Yeah if you have the yeah if you have the sound if yeah yeah I mean if you have speakers anybody can get it sure. It's all her, yeah. Yeah yeah exactly yeah. Yeah exactly. The matzohs on it yeah yeah yeah. Yeah, let's see. Yeah. Yeah. Yeah no. Right. Uh, yeah I can't believe that. Yeah yeah. Uh, yeah yeah yeah. Yeah, I've got see all those books the same size yeah yeah. Yeah. So that's really interesting, yeah. Isn't that funny, yeah? Yeah yeah yeah. Yeah, um, yeah I yeah no it all sounds interesting to me, um, you know I really love this place. Yeah, well I was Bar Mitzvahed at the, uh, wailing wall, yeah yeah. Yeah. Yeah yeah. Alright you guys. Right. Yeah, how's everything going. Yeah great. Great great. Yeah. Yeah yeah we don't. Right. Right. Yeah, well, alright listen. Right, right, yeah. Yeah, alright. Yeah. Yeah yeah I think they're really easy to read. Yeah, I heard she did it yeah. Yeah. Yeah. Yeah. Yeah. Yeah, I miss you guys. OK? Yeah. Uh, Power PC, uh, 8500. Yeah, really? Right. Uh huh. Right. Right. Yeah. Right. Right. Right. 7.5.2, right. Uh huh. Really? Uh. Yeah yeah. Yeah. Uh, yeah. Yeah. Uh. Yeah. Yeah. Uh huh. Yeah. Um, whoa! Yeah, it looks like. Yeah. Right. Right. Cheryl look at this guy, yeah. Yeah, see you later. Yeah. Yeah, she's so sandy. Right. Cheryl. Yeah, uh, I don't know. Yeah yeah, no it's good. Yeah. Yeah. Yeah. Yeah I was, yeah, I'm glad I missed that. Yeah. Oh yeah. Right. Find out, yeah. Anyway, yeah, c'mon. Yeah, it's really catchy. Where's... yeah, you guys are tiny. Cheryl. Uh, impotent. Who tried to, yeah. Yeah. Yeah yeah. Yeah. Yeah. Yeah, we should. Yeah, it is. Yeah, maybe nobody's inside. Yeah OK, yeah. You already know, yeah. Yeah, it was packed. Yeah. Yeah it was Ubu, yeah. Cheryl, yeah. Yeah. Uh, around? Uh huh. RISD was cool, yeah. Yeah. What we're thinking, yeah. Yeah. Yeah, the business section. Yeah, PDF. Yeah I did yeah they have a website. Yeah. Beth, yeah. Yeah, you're not. Yeah. Yeah, well I like guys with big noses. Uh, Long Island. Yeah. Yeah. Right right right. Yeah. Right? Oh yeah. Yeah, I know. Yeah, that's true. I telnet, yeah. Yeah, it's easy, yeah. Yeah yeah yeah. I mean, yeah, sure. Yeah and then work on Panix yeah yeah yeah yeah yeah, well sure. Yeah, no no no. 6 oh oh yeah. Yeah. Yeah, maybe. Yeah yeah. Yeah. I like Daniel, yeah. Yeah, yeah. Keep, yeah. Yeah. Yeah. It's very cool, yeah yeah. Yeah yeah no. Yeah, it isn't hard. Yeah. Yeah, yeah. It is, yeah. Yeah, embarrassing. Yeah yeah. Yeah yeah. Great. Yeah. Yeah. Yeah. Yeah, oh it is. Yeah, look at that. Yeah, she's a trip. Yeah. Right? Yeah yeah. Yeah, it's a depressing building. Yeah. Yeah. Yeah. Yeah. Yeah. Yeah, oh it is. Yeah, look at that. Yeah, she's a trip. Yeah. Right? Yeah yeah. Yeah.

Friday

Alright. Yeah, there's no food. Right. Yeah yeah. Yeah, it's easier. Right right. Yeah. Alright. Alright. Alright. Yeah. Yeah. Uh huh. I mean, yeah. Alright? Oh yeah. Yeah. Yeah, it's really good. Yeah. Yeah. Alright! Yeah. Yeah. Yeah, look, she's smiling. Yep gonna stay with them, yeah, that's right. Yeah. Uh. Yeah. Yeah. Yeah, don't dawdle. Yeah yeah yeah. OK, yeah yeah. Alright. Yeah. Yeah, I'm telling ya. Yeah. Alright. Yeah. Yeah yeah yeah. Yeah I love that. Um, yeah yeah. Yeah, hello. Yeah. Yeah. Yeah. Right. Yeah, he's pegged. Yeah, we're ready, yeah. Yeah. Yeah, several years ago. Yeah yeah. Yeah, we got one. Yeah, that sounds great. Right right. It was Roanoke, yeah. Very much, yeah. Yeah. Yeah. Yeah. Yeah. Really, you know, I think it's, yeah yeah. Yeah it's insubstantial. Yeah, well. Yeah. Yeah. Yeah. Yeah. Yeah. Right. Yeah. Yeah. Um, yeah yeah yeah we will we will start. I'm gonna I'm gonna pick. Yeah. Yeah. Oh, yeah. Alright. Oh, yeah. Yeah, you'll enjoy Bruce. Yeah, alright, yeah, I'm gonna go to Aikido tonight I hope. Alright! Alright? Alright. Alright? Alright. Yeah, you think so? Alright, yeah. Right. Yeah. Yeah yeah yeah. I only got everything from you, yeah yeah. Yeah. Yeah. Uh, yeah I have the original here, yeah. Ah, yeah, aw. Yeah, she's seven. Yeah. Uh huh. Yeah. Yeah. Back food, yeah. Yeah, they love dogs here. Yeah, that's a hassle. Yeah, no. I believe so, yeah. Student discount, yeah. Yeah, definitely do. Yeah. Yeah. Yeah. Yeah, where is this? Right. Yeah, who wrote it? Yeah yeah. Uh huh. Yeah, oh yeah, really. Yeah. Yeah. Yeah? Yeah. Yeah yeah. Yeah. Yeah, it is time consuming. Yeah yeah I like that. Oh yeah? Yeah. Yeah, right right. Yeah, she's really nice. Yeah. Yeah yeah. Yeah yeah yeah. Yeah. It's really a. Yeah. Yeah, no. Yeah. Yeah yeah. Right. Yeah. Yeah. Yeah. Yeah. Right. Yeah, thanks a lot. Yeah. Right, well that's yeah. I mean what... yeah. For you, yeah yeah. Yeah. Right. Yeah. Right. Yeah. Yeah. I'm sure, yeah. Yeah. Yeah. Yeah. Yeah, I like her work. Yeah. Yeah. Right. Right. Right? Yeah. Yeah. Yeah, yeah. Yeah. Yeah, it's it's really. Right? Yeah, they're good. Yeah. Yeah, Graham's a good guy. Yeah. Yeah. Yeah. Yeah. Yeah. Yeah. Yeah, Alix told me. Yeah. Yeah. Really stop or, yeah? Yeah, all.

Yeah. Yeah. It's yeah. All right. Huh? Yeah. Yeah, it's really weird. Yeah, it's a 10:20. Yeah, they're nice dogs. Yeah. Yeah. Yeah yeah yeah. Oh yeah. Yeah great. Yeah. Yeah, right. All right. All right. All right. Yeah. Yeah, no reports. Yeah. 28. Right. Right. Yeah. Yeah. Yeah. Right. Right. Yeah. Yeah. Huh? Yeah. Cheryl. All right. Yeah, just fuck it. All right. Yeah yeah yeah. Right. Yeah. Yeah Bruce knows it. Max. Yeah, those are shells. Nice throw, Cheryl. Yeah yeah. Yeah, me too. Yeah, they're very nice. Yeah, uh huh. Yeah. Yeah escapade. Right. Yeah. Yeah. Yeah. Yeah, should be really nice. Yeah. All right. Yeah. Yeah. It's getting there, yeah. Yeah, what's going on? Yeah, that's amazing. Right. Ah, yeah. Yeah. Yeah. Yeah to like what? All right, all right. Oh yeah? Yeah there was. Oh yeah? Yeah. Yeah. You know, yeah. Ceramics, yeah yeah. All right. Yeah, why don't you? Yeah, that's me. What an idiot, yeah. Yeah. Yeah, he's pretty evil, yeah. Oh yeah, oh yeah. Yeah. Yeah. Yeah. Yeah. Yeah yeah. Yeah, it's very exciting. Yeah. Yeah. I love opera, yeah. Yeah, I love it. Yeah. Yeah, good child. Yeah. I see, yeah. Yeah. Max. Max. Yeah. Yeah. Yeah, I feel good. I did, yeah. Yeah. Yeah. Yeah, yeah. Yeah. Yeah, what about them? Yeah? Oh yeah? Why? Yeah yeah. Yeah, me too. Yeah. Yeah, yeah. Yeah yeah big mall. Yeah. Yeah. Right. Yeah. Max. All right. Yeah yeah all right yeah. Yeah, they're like loafers. Yeah? Yeah, so was I. Yeah. Yeah. Yeah, Cheryl's pretty upset about it. Yeah still, huh? All right all right. All right. Yeah. Yeah. Yeah. Uh huh. Yeah. Yeah. Yeah. Yeah yeah. Right here. Yeah. Yeah. Yeah, this is wild. Yeah. MTV, yeah. Yeah. Yeah. Yeah. Yeah. Yeah, we'll talk, yeah, let's let's yeah, I will. Yeah, I tried. Yeah yeah. Yeah, they're cool. Yeah. Yeah. Yeah we're gonna make a 4:44. Yeah yeah, our is better. All right. All right. You got a yeah yeah yeah. All right? Yeah. Yeah. Yeah. All right... Yeah yeah yeah. Yeah, let us know. All right. All right. All right. Yeah yeah. Yeah. It was nice, yeah. Right right right. Right right. The work looks great, yeah. Right right. Yeah, no no. You're right. Yeah I yeah I don't know. Yeah I yeah I don't know. Yeah, yeah. Yeah, me neither. On Church they used to, yeah yeah. Yeah, no they're small. Yeah. Oh, yeah, Cat. Right, I like Cat, yeah. Right right. Yeah. Right, right. Yeah, yeah. Yeah. Yeah, Caracas connection. Yeah yeah. Oh yeah? Oh yeah, we're dishing. Right right right. Yeah yeah. You're right. Yeah, well I was. Yeah, they used to. Yeah. Right. Yeah. Babe, yeah. Yeah. Yeah, the Milk Bar, right. Yeah yeah. Yeah. Oh yeah. Right right right. Yeah. Yeah. Yeah. Yeah. Yeah, we do, yeah. Yeah. Yeah. Yeah. Yeah. Right right. Right. Yeah. All right. Yeah. Yeah yeah. Yeah. Yeah. Yeah. Yeah. Where is that, yeah. Yeah. Right. Yeah. Yeah. Right. Yeah. Uh uh. Yeah. Everybody once, yeah yeah. Oh my god, yeah. Yeah. Doing yeah yeah. Right. Right. Right. Yeah. Well, yeah, but then yeah, like yeah honey you look good. Right. Yeah, she's plastic, yeah. Yeah. Cheryl, Cheryl. Yeah, where? Provisions, yeah. Yeah. By boat, yeah. Uh huh. All right. It really, yeah, what's? Yeah. Yeah, these are these. Yeah. All right. Yeah. Yeah yeah. Yeah, I know. Yeah. Right right right right. Yeah. Yeah, we love Gong. Yeah, I, yeah. Yeah. Yeah, we're done. Yeah. Yeah. Yeah yeah yeah. Yeah, I don't have it yeah. Yeah. All right. Nice. Yeah. Yeah yeah. Yeah. Yeah. Yeah. Yeah. All right. Yeah. All right. Yeah, yeah. Yeah. Uh, god. Yeah yeah. Yeah. Yeah. Yeah yeah. Yeah, yeah. Yeah yeah.

Sunday

Yeah. Yeah. Uh huh. Right? Right. Alright. Right? Yeah. Yeah, yeah. Yeah, they're alright. Yeah. Right. Yeah. Yeah. Yeah. Yeah, Ginny. Yeah yeah. Alright. Yeah? Cheryl. Yeah. Yeah? Uh huh. Yeah? Right? Alright. Yeah. Alright, well. Yeah, it's so pretty. Yeah. What? Yeah? Cheryl. Chagall, yeah. It certainly wasn't the, uh uh, the Jewish show, yeah. Yeah, yeah. Alright. Alright. Yeah yeah, that's the that's the famous, uh, place down there over there. Yeah. Yeah. Yeah. Yeah? Yeah. Yeah. Yeah. It's really nice, yeah. Yeah, finally. Yeah, it's always stuffy. Yeah. Uh, for four. Cheryl. Yeah. Yeah, yeah I think it's croquet. Yeah. It yeah. Yeah, so soft. Yeah but it's actually a table and sure, yeah. Cheryl? Yeah yeah, uh, toasted dry please and and a, uh, coffee. Uh huh. Yeah. Yeah, that might be nice. Yeah. I love it, yeah. Yeah, let's go somewhere else. With Ann though, yeah. Yeah. Somebody was, yeah. Yeah. Yeah. Oh, yeah. Yeah. Oh, yeah. Yeah. Yeah. Yeah. Uh, how so? Yeah. Yeah. Yeah yeah. Right. Yeah. Yeah, no but its... Uh, no. Yeah, a little bit a little bit of drool. Right. Yeah. Yeah yeah that was really, that was really idiotic. Bruce. Alright. Yeah, it is. Good, yeah, OK. Uh, it was OK, yeah. Yeah. Yeah. Cheryl. Yeah. Way more academic, yeah yeah. Cheryl. Cheryl. Yeah. Hi guys. Yeah. Yeah yeah, that's right. Yeah. Yeah yeah. Some old standard, yeah. Yeah, he's interesting. Yeah. Yeah. Yeah, look. Right Nick? Yeah, I love yeah. OK, yeah. Yeah. Pretty rich stuff, yeah. Yeah. Yeah. Yeah, of course. Yeah, right. Yeah, mote is amazing. Yeah. Yeah yeah yeah. Yeah. Interesting, yeah. Yeah. Yeah, that's right. Yeah yeah no that's. Yeah. Yeah. Yeah but not Marjorie. Yeah. Yeah. Right. Yeah, it's good. Yeah. You like talk, yeah. Bruce? Yeah. Yeah. Yeah, last time we were out. Yeah. Yeah, he failed. East Village, yeah. Right. Yeah. Yeah. Pretty much, yeah. Yeah. Yeah, completely impoverished. Yeah, no that's better. Yeah. Yeah. Right. Yeah, it's pretty good. Yeah, right, yeah. Yeah yeah yeah. Yeah. Yeah yeah. Yeah. Yeah. Sorry guy. Yeah, they're very funny. Uh huh. Cheryl. Alright dogs. Yeah. Yeah, it's like 7:15. Yeah, she's beautiful. Yeah, she is. Baron, yeah. Yeah. Yeah, they're terrific. Yeah. Yeah, I got three. C'mon guys c'mon guys. Yeah. Yeah. Yeah. Right? Yeah, you're right, she's gonna bark here. Uh huh. Yeah, who is he? Nice guy? Right? Yeah, I got them. Yeah. Yeah. Little rusty? Yeah, let's get new wheels. Yeah, it's pretty, isn't it? Yeah, you know what? Yeah go on. Yeah. Yeah. Yeah, aren't they? Nice. Yeah, her trail. Right. Yeah, c'mon. Yeah yeah. Yeah, she's no philosopher. Bruce? Yeah. Yeah yeah. Yeah. Uh, I think it's... yeah... work... yeah. Yeah. Yeah. Yeah. Right. Right. Right. Yeah. Uh huh. Right. Yeah. Right? Uh huh yeah yeah well. Uh huh. Uh huh. Uh huh. Uh huh. Yeah yeah yeah. Uh huh. Uh huh. Yeah. Right. Right. Yeah, get in touch. Yeah, something like that, yeah, it's impossible. Yeah yeah. Yeah. Yeah. Well. Right. Yeah. Right. Yeah. Cheryl?

SEHNSUCHT

"ful oft þæt earn bigeal"

Might a few /
    suffocate? HERE
    . Like a clock
    stroke—   Stranger sa
llies wending wanton
    forth freedomly   Frate
rnally, I'm afraid. Na
turally, I've told y
    Well-descr
    ibed by Ne
    wman as a
"psychoact
ive, hallu
    ci ou. L
    'm carr
    ying on
    this c
onversa
    tion be
cause o
    f my pl
    an t   o disinteg
    rate you with
a ray-gun, or
Reaganomics. S
    trappe   nogenic neocortex p
    ulsator," the Dreamachine
    is basically d to the
    bedstand, wyws (very
different from eyes) w
anderin around aboun
ding inegenuously w
    ith wisdomish cousi
    n c a cylind
    er with irr
egularly pa
tterned, ye

t symmetac
al, c   cant

ankerous a
 midst the
 merely cur
ious. Rath
er than re
tire   g to and from corners
. He calls for kittens
 to tickle his deft
    feet.

Snow is fa
 lling. The   the quest
   ion, perspire in the
residual insurrecti
 o ustoms that theo
critically contai
     n croutons. Power
  prospect
  s cover
  comforta
 bly sati
n suburb
  s instant   utouts which sp
    ins at 80 r.p.m around
 a h igh
   -watta
 ge lig
ht. Wh
  en sta
  red at
  in   n. Efforts effe
  cts—the merely
slogan. Hi gh b
   row as teletyp
   e. HERE. Class
   Act you—r   tly in
clined. Fragmented
 fixes gear gradu
   ally senatorial,
  superiority fre
  netically   Roman Cathol
ic Church gives itself

a face lift.

A bu   a da
  rk room with the eyes clos
    ed, it produces a strobosc
      opi   c "flicke
  r" effect on
      the eyelids
    , sometimes   farced
  . Great gnomes are
      ardently u   econ
 sider that tri
 p to Miami? On
  e purple Marxi
    sm to another   nderstand
 ing understatement, in
 telligently it
      : "I prefer
      their safety
      caps." HERE
      . Guesstimat
      e—oo   oh, I hate that wor
      d. Creation date of
      fferfly (very diff
      erent from a butte
 rfly) wanders into
      the   erating. Bourgevinea b
 attles wage wrathfu
      the person dat
    e. Knute takes
      the garbage out
      and says Hey-   lly ove
      r overdetermined pren
 atal politic
  orphanage, w
      hich is not
 liberal, and
 plants its
      w   king. And androi
      dal philippic phi
      losophies gradi   ate gar
      gantual entrepreneuria
 I encounters. Frame th
 e la   ho Sally!

81

—she's jus
t turned the
coroner. With
the bricks.
causing i
ntense vi
sions and
frighten
ing perce
p   me, / big th
e game, / fix
the quaranti
ne / abo   Her
boredom is ex
quisite and e
xcessive and   tions that "
approximate or surpass t
hose ve the lane, / (a
scrape against / the P
tolemaic sky), / bru
sh a stick / against
the leaves. How po   et kiss on
the marm. Practice this kiss
she would like someone to
speak to her. "Prize alla
h   found in
a dream st
ate." Accor
ding to Dav
i   or, how rich, how
abject, how august,
how complic   d
Woodard, who
built Cobain
's Dreamachin
e as ate, how
wonderful,
is man! How
passing won
/ I'm
blue /
back
off/
from t

his hu

e."

Mar   der, he who made him such!
Who centered in our make such
   strange extremes! How d
ifferent natures marvelo
   usly mixed
and yo
u will
 be ad
mitted
, she
says.
      Es   s attacked all o
   ur verbs—now we
   mumble anthems of
sta   ! Connection exquisi
  te of distant worlds! Di
sting   we
    ll as th
   e deluxe
  , all-me
tal unit
  include
d in " Ports
of Entry," t
  he Dreamachi
ne's 10-flas
  h-per   timate the amount
  of ribbon it would take
  to type out   -sec
  ond flicker is t
ranslated by the
optic nerve the
  entire sycophant
  constitution. The
  meta   uish'd link in being
's endless chain! Midway
  from n   sis. This bagel won
't do anything in
I heels a
  nd toes s

  crape aga
  inst the

              tile floo
     rs. Wha   into a 1
0-hertz pulse si
          gnal—close to
     that w   t
          ? it is
     making u
           s believ
     e.

Bu
       t wh   myh
     ands. A
       healthy
         surreali
         sm hijac
     ked the
     tenn   othing to the deity! A be
          am ethereal sullied, an
     is cou
       rts. P
          remier
     e Stri
          ch—
     that b
     aby tr
     ap. Al
          lusion
       t   hich occurs in the dream sta
       te. Because the brain c
an't accommodate b
       oth its normal ope
          r   d absorbt! T
       hough sullied
            and dishonou
            red, still di
            at would be f
            ound there bu
       t a bunch of
            igloos   o Ashbery
          counting his da

     ndelion fin   gers?
     Who doesn't like
       the crucifixion –

– it's a ki   vine!
    Dim milliature o
    f grearness abso
    lute! An heir of
    glory   te? Charles Sheeler p
hotographed the factories.
    ating frequency of 5 to
    6 hertz and the newly
    introduced l
    Charles Sh
      eeler also   .
    paintinge
      d and draw
      inged the
    factories   ! A fr
ail child of du
    st! Helpless im
      mortal! I   0-he
rtz wavelength
    h simultaneou
    sly, and also
      becau   with minor literary fix
tures retired among them?

He
 trigge
rs the
    dynam
   o with
   his a
 shtray
: the
    abun   dance, the dancing,
    the cowardices, I   nsect i
   nfinite! To you! whoever
  you are, w
se the
    10-he
   rtz si
gnal i

  s so o
  verpow
    erring,   t
   he entir
  e neocor

tex soon
   gives i
   tself   over to th
 e higher frequent
 cy, effectively
   putting the   . The lami
   nated Howl. Wintering
 in my cabi   n on a hil
 l, where the deer are
   frothy with poetry   ndices
   of a carnival described
      within its profusion
   viewer into a dream
      state. Wrong "notes
 "   are left as they are rathe
 r than erased, though the
      —unschooled, they wh
 ore no backpack
   s.

 H
   onorifi
   c quatr
   ntine.
   Sibylli
 ne trow
 els. Gr
      easy su
 n ri   right ones
   do eventually g
   et "played"   herever you are!
   (But I know where you are!)
   The   . Interrogated,
 the proteins survi
      ve under   in most cases.
   This results in a repet
 itiveness an   d
   a halting, s

 taccato gestu
   re reminiscen
 t of a stutte
 r   re's Durer's "
 Nemesis" naked
            on her sphere o

ver the little   the
microscope but an
            imate more the sun
      light that, furt   herm
ore, only animates h
is face. His familia
          r   er's effort to get out w
      hat he wants to say. Thus,
            Wil   liams: "Americ
      an poetry was on i
      ts way   fa
            ce const
      ructed l
ike a ji
            gsaw, it
      self. (T
            he fruit
      s and fo
      r   se. Makar you dood
le! It's almost Sum
            mer and   town by
      the river—ex
            cept she's too o
      ld.   There's a dancing burgess
      by Tenier and Villon's ma
      to great distinction –
      – when the blight of El
      iot's popular
      All—it
            is.

J
      ust anoth
            er Americ
      an poet r
ubbi   verse fell pon—u
pon the gasping unive

ng his
            fuzzy g
      enitals
            agains
t every
      thing   he loves.

You've t
        aken benighted gossip a ste
            p too itres
s—after
    he'd gone
        bald and
            was shin p
    ocked and
        toot   rsities—who had
            N8t hadN8t hadn't tast
        ed the   Thames water
            for nearly a hundr
ed years." By di   ks of
an assault on classica
            l volumetrics
        hless:
        she t
        hat ha
            d him
                ducked
                in th
    e sewa
        ge dra
            in.   .) Wan
                dering am
            ong the t
erminolog
            y culled
        fro   srupting
            fluency an
    d coherence
        avail   fa
r. You ar
            e touchh
        g yoursel
        f with a

        dirty spa
    tu   Then there's that miller's
daughter of   m popular maga
        zines and essays, he fant
    asi   zes am
ong thc G
            reeks of
his new f

ound pavi
lion. Hat
red es   la. The Taois
t pops, which makes
me jump—up. On t
he seve   able to
them Williams a
nd Miller attem
pt to get
nth da
y, I p
ut dow
n my p
enicil
lin an
d rest
ed   in touc
h with wha
t that coh
erence exc
ludes   capes from the ey
es of the auditors   "buttock
s broad and breastes high." S
omething of Nietzsche
, "the chaos agains
t which that patter
n was concei   . b
ut palms raise
their leaves be
hind t   , someth
ing of the goo
d Samaritan, s
omething of th
e devil
ved."
Althou

gh sup
erfici
ally t
he pic
ture   may look like a
Cubist collage, the
rei   s n
o inter
est her

e in st

 structure

or the

dimens

ions of   . The Ty

ro wears red un

derwear. (We ar

e all little   girls

.) Tubelet the boo

by. What is it abo

ut, you ask? T

himself,—

can cut a cap

er of a fash   ion

, my fashion! H

ey you, the dan

ce! SL,uat. Leap

.   time and space; it is o

bsessionally, im

hem, framing

them, expla

ining them,

and unwittin   gly in their

bafflement they modify th

e limning of their mim

etic pathology. Sleep

is the res   Hops

to the left.

Chin—ha!—

sideways! S   he

sleeping gem

of the millio

aire. Is it ar

t, or is it fi   patiently sexual

. But its sexuality is

tand up, stand up ma

bonne! you'll break m

y backbon   le-o-fax (Halifax),

you ask? Seventy-five hundr

ed conf

e. So

again!

—an

d so f

orth t

ill we

　　　　're sw

　　　　eat so

　　　　aked.

GET YO　　　　　　　　　　　　　　U ON / give roger bel

　　ls / eyes down now / think

　　　slips randy

　　　　　idences

　　　　later... The soft h

　of a wheezing soun

　　　　d f　　　in in which

　he can find the

　contentment　　ills

　　　the stadium. The

　　talent scouts are

　　　troubled　　　that

　　is preserving

　　　　his june bug.

　　　　　　　　　with omissions, deci

　　　　sions, correcting　　　without a su

　bject. It is as though this pi

　　　　cture were　　　　　crying out for a L

　　　eda and the Swan, or a Nymph

　　and Shephard

　　, or a Venus

　　, to be give

　　n a form. Bu

　　t ther　　　/ haven't we swam / b

　efore so terrible / with nam

　　　es face　　　　Holograms

　　are not people,

　　　　nor steeples peop

les. Paddi　　　minors. [...

Tr-tr-tr-tr...] A poss

　　um, he fling　　　　e is nobody

　　to call that form into b

eing, nobody to es a

　　　re not economies tha

　　t divide the lot amo

　　　　ng slow wage sl

aves. G

　　atherer

　　　s are e

91

arners
—citi
zens in
leisur
e— name it and sep
arate it from Picass
o by believing in it
. Wha t Picasso is expressing
here becomes absurd because
there s a sneaker toward
it. Apathy. For instance,
"walnuts ch oke the trees."
Or, "Everybody's too busy re
surr s / such g
lasses on / si
mply sally doe
s / who now sn
e is nothing to resist hi
m: neither the subject,
aky /
high r
ise ru
ffs /
coo to
rucks
acks /
physi
que recombine
in Beulah wary
of thc remot says it / we'
ll hold thumbs / stamp t
nor h
is awa
reness

of re
ality
as und
erstoo
d by o
the rs. Wi
thout suc
h resista
nce the w
hole of S

ha   e control. Solitudes dri
       ft warily in high re   he o
dour / dawn is heavy / m
              ike's your bimbo / t
              kespea
                  re's L
         ear wo
uld be
         no mo
         re tha
           n ad e
             ath-r   hat shaver did / with t
his sponger / as loveliest f
    eelings   ecting Jack Spicer
    to read new books o   f poetry." |
       Empathy. That's like saying
                 Nixon didn't
         s patter
ns that
                never st
    rike the
    diamond
      , nor pu
    sh off.   The meaning
    of this continues
    when the scro   / flood the hu
         ffaloes Hwilum ylfete song d
yde   ic me to gomene, ga
            netes hleopor ond h
           set o
           ut to
be ope
ratic.
            Ipane

    me. Am
          idst t
      h   ll is
    enact
         ed. Pr
edeces
      sors k
      indly
      are as
        ked to

lea   attle. They
ought to be some
how the core of
a langua
uilpan s
weg fore
hleahto
r wera m
æw sing   ge, ide
ntifiable by t
racing its his
tory backwa   ve. Or fl
oat over the Macy's
Day Parade.

This
is   my Latin mo
vhig outfit. T
hese are my ch
arged synapses
, emit   in
g signals
at a fas
ter rate
than norm
al   Man. This is a book
I rate very highly. Sta
nding   rd. Mid-19th ce
ntury England abounde
d in amia   ble enthusias
ts for Saxon roots. Th
e "fin   ende fore medodrince.
Stormas þær stancl   e curious

.

a lifer loamed. Wid A riddm
from tine Mormon.
ifu beotan; þær
him stearn onc
wæð, isig   e
old fellow
/ named Fur
nivall" (18
25-1910) wh
ose repute

I   s alluded to in the Pisan C
          antos [...]; Bridges (who sa
      id of   the old words
          'We'll get them al
  l back') admired D
      oughty, mu
              ch of whos
      e Dawn of
          Britain Po
  und read a
              lo   .   ud to Yeats one wartime win
          ter; Doughty I   n turn wa
              s indebted to the Speec
          hcraft (i.e. Gramma   feþera; fu
  l oft þæt earn bigeal, urigfe
              þera; ne ænig hleomæ   a
  lone in the rain, high
      on several humped bac
          ks, permanent   A
      midst the war
              s, their pros
  trate "g"   r) of William Barnes,
          who proposed sunp   , the codi
  cil snored. A barbazon type
          of 100   rint or flamepri
          nt to replace photogra
          ph,   t as an obsessional ev
  ening fixation, the retir
          questions. Fluxed fax
          ly. Vulcan, he rem   sleep
      stow for dormitory, and
              pitches of suchness for
  deg   rees of compar
      ison, drawing alw

  ays on   ga feas
      ceaftig ferð f
              refran meahte.
          Tak /   embered the
      dance gig, the l
      eather thongs. No
          stri   ed librarian stuffs hi
  s pipe. That is the cinema
          . That is   str
          en / quar / de
      velo / veron /

pin / antlik
/ restor Comme   the "wordstore
    s of the landfolk."
ls date
    d all t
                he cele
brities
    . Garbo
        nzo dip
            wasted
            the cu   j
        e descend
ais des F
leuves im
                passibles
, J   tlery. The
                canonical wa
    s the heat of
the c   onvers
    ation, the d
            evolution th
                e meat. A th
            ousand times
        I   e ne me sentais plus guidé
    par les haleurs :   Des P
eaux-Rouges criards les
        avaient pris pour
the fac
    ade of
            the Hou
                se of(
    broken)
            Parli   have wondered where

.

                    I put that ice-pick, since
                                my nails have to
            go (tobogganed). C
                hinee.   Not
                hing is so
        easy as r
            emembering
                    the last
            time you p
                ut yo   ur knee
            caps in the c

heese.

A g
        land under th
         e peanuts b
    owl with
                hyperboli
         c amours.
                Their ec
                riture   cibles Les a
        yant cloués nus aux
                poteaux   de couleurs.
        J'etais insoucieux d
                e tous les équipage   s, Porteu
            r de blés flamands et de cot
                on   a lox. Falls the net, chink
        . Insatiable parade   am
                ent. This is Wittgens
        tein's Theory of Pain

            .

                    Ordinarily, I'm aloo
        f.

Fraternally, I'm af
        rai   d.

Nat
                urally, I've I
            told you.

Something
        contagious i
        n s   uburb
            an airs
                bleats p
        ontifica
    ting aga
                ins   gms of transcend
            ence relegated to t
                he count [CLAN   K
        ] of a harm [CL
            ANK] beat [CLAN

97

                    K] white out of
its [CL.   s anglais. Qu
    and avec mes haleurs
        ont fini ces tapages
                    Les   ANK] essence. The
                    wraith of this snee
    ze in the wilds—s
                t strategic
        paradise m
        aneuvers. A
                fork in th
e lion of   the road te
        lls the tinsel town:
    "Pragmatics are weepy
                    .
                                        " Historicism fa
            ltering in the di
                ve to   s
                    obriety
                , they
                        grind t
                        heir te
        eth, me
                    ek, t   o
                    me sor
    t of p
                erfume
        on th
                    e marg
ins. D
    iddle

daddle
    --   Fleuves m'ont lais
            sé descendre où je vo
                    ulais. Dans le
    my aunty's one c
                ontribution to m
        y readi   s clapotemen
        ts furieux des maré
                        es, Moi, l'autre hi
            ve   ng list. Where t
                    he fish never swea
        r. Anudda o   he slow plowing
    down billions when they've
        understood   r, plus sourd
            que les cerveaux d'enf

98

ants, Je courrus !   veraci

ty. Track this spot to th

e edge of tow

n, to a hut

with windo

ws. Monocle

s are for s

ale in the

galle   ry.

They t

hank and

think the

re's spir

als in th

e wi   ne ride

's da bus-a

. How about

the Declar

ation of In

depen   dget of the if

fy expanding univer

se, maps contendin

dence font?

Et les Péni

nsules démar

rée   g for the crown in mi

xed doubles, cartog   raphic

winners fixing that ball

point Zen.

Afterwa   s N'on

t pas subi tohu-bohus plus t

riomphants.   r

ds, it was

the weeke

nd—you

called me

on the cel

l   phone but you diale

d Stonehenge. Healthi

ly, not immediate   ely.

KLUGE: A MEDITATION

"I am sitting in a room…"—Alvin Lucier

First Season: Communiqués

჻

I guess what I mean to say to you is that I have always felt
that I don't want, or am afraid, to make choices in my life,
but rather prefer the *emotions* to make them for me, whatever
one might decide "emotions" are, finally. I'm as comfortable
thinking they are exterior to what I, even incorrectly, call
my body and its relations, or can be corollary emanations of
them. They might flare behind me brightly like scarves, like
the scarves that decapitated Isadora Duncan -- "affectations
can be dangerous," Gertrude Stein famously quipped -- when a
trail got caught in the spokes of a wheel of the car she was
driving in and snapped her neck. Or they might be kept close
to the heart, in private, the nesting bird in the breast, to
which one turns only on occasion and without causing anybody
to notice: in annoyance, or in sorrow. A poem without "fuck"
in it is like the proverbial day without sunshine, as Stefan
not quite as famously said. The relevance of his remark with
what I am writing now might never be clear, but I thought to
include it anyway, showing my love for you is not just brain
matter in the platonic undercurrents of my psyche, but is as
well a pact of desire body and "soul," imagining I have one.

I know what I mean to write right now is that I often feel I
don't like, or want, to make changes in my life, but instead
that I need *passions* to obviate them for me. But I doubt the
"passions" are a terribly modern concept this day and age. I
am as happy thinking they are exterior to myself, like goons
I could meet at a park who ruin a pleasant twilit night, the
gnats playing with my hair on the dry softball field several
Narragansetts past returning. In reaction, I elect my body a
situation, and I am simply an emanation of it. It might flow
behind me like princely dandruff, like the flock of dandruff
that humiliated me in grammar school -- "affectations can be
dangerous," Gertrude Stein might chime in -- as a seborrheic
scurf hung on the spokes of the wheel of my maturity, making
this growing man a mere blip on the sexual screen of puberty
among my funky, female friends. They were a car driving away
snapping my neck. They are near to my heart, in private, the
bird interred in my chest, the cooking turkey in the holiday
oven of the self, which one turns so as not to cause another
bird to burn. A poem without "fuck" in it is like a summer's
day without rain, if for a second you hold yourself to love.

ॐ

I have something to say to you, but I am trying to write the
words down quickly, about making changes in the way I write,
since I need *being* to enact *writing* even when merely *typing*,
since, however "posthuman," I need *soul*. I'm not sure "soul"
is a sexy, chic concept finally, unlike "Cheetohs," a modest
American food as malnutritious as it is suitable for framing
smashed on a wall. I am happy thinking they are not inside a
stomach. I like goons, Narragansetts, the proverbial days of
fucking, and Battlestar Galactica. Pretentiously I call soul
a *situation*, and I am simply an emanation of it: an animated
dandruff I mean to find affirming, as Gertrude Stein opined:
"Affectations can be dangerous." But she was a prissy hiccup
on the prepubescent sexual screen of puberty among my funky,
female friends. They weigh on my heart, proverbial chicks in
my chicken breast, the cooling turd in the Frigidaire patent
of the self, to which one turns without making anything else
stir. A poem without "smut" in it is an odorless, plain Jane
day without pain, but not if you lease yourself to love. The
Byronic racer of the psyche flips into gear as I write this.
In service stairs the sweet corruption thrives, a poet said.

I have something to write, but I don't know how to start. It is about making changes in the way I write, since I know you will read this -- a change in reading. I need *seeing* to back *writing* especially when "typing," since, though more modern, more robust, than earlier releases of myself, I need *traffic* with my past. I need *stability*. I am not sure "stability" is a terribly modern concept finally, unlike "Cheetohs." I feel suitable for framing smashed on a wall, but this realization is, uh, limiting. I like goons, Narragansetts, Debussy, sex, and Battlestar Galactica. Battlestar Galactica, the new one, is a situation, and I am only an emanation of it, confirming Gertrude Stein when she pedantically observed: "Affectations can be dangerous." She was a ludic prude, despite very true, on the homosexual screen of prepubescent tomfoolery among my funky, female friends. It lolls in my soul like a proverbial cholesterol in the arteries of my chicken breast, a pellucid turd in a recently patented alphabet soup, causing no one an omen, foretastes of cruelty. A poem without "puck" is like a day without sex, if the provincial racist charges to special effects. In service stairs the sweet corruption thrives, uh.

❧

I have something to, uh, write but, uh, yeah, I don't really know how, uh, how to say this but, uh, it's about making, uh you know, changes in the way, since I know you will, uh yeah read this, like I need *being*, uh, reading, I don't know man, even *writing*, since, uh, though modern, robust, like earlier releases, dude I'm *stoked*, myself. I need my, yeah er, past? I need stability (woah). Haha, I am not sure stability is so cool, like "Cheetohs." Dude, I feel framed, smashed lol on a wall, but this realization is, uh, proverbial? Narragansetts now! Debussy, sex, and Battlestar Galactica now! I am a, uh, a situation, and I am only, uh, also a byproduct, uh like in chem lab, dude, oh, uh, like in the *Matrix*. Like, confirming Gertrude Stein when she shit-facedly confided: "Affectations can be dangerous." She sucked, but was so right. And I'm gay and prepubescent, uh, yeah! You are a funky, fertile friend. You loll in my soul like cholesterol, *hungh!* in the arteries of my breast-patient self, *hungh!*, causing no hurt, no pain, uh, yeah like I *like* you. A poem with "fuck" in it, AWESOME. What are you doing now? Want to, uh, hang out in the service stairs at Steinart? I read books by John Ashbery there, huh.

I have something to say to you, uh, yeah. But I'm really not good at talking about things, uh. Duh. I suck. I like barely know how to make anything happen, uh, no. Changes, you know, in the way I live, you know, like I need *being-in-my-life* to know what to say about life. I don't know, writing... sucks. It's hardly modern, robust, like fighting wars or traveling. I'm not excited about life, myself. I need a past to enliven my present, you know? I don't need stability *at all*. I'm not sure stability should (like Cheetohs) even be legal. (Haha). Sipping from a very large glass of very inexpensive Vendange Chardonnay, dude, listening to Debussy and writing this, uh, I feel alarmed. But this realization is the proverbial spunk on an analyst's clock, and I am only an afterthought, like I can't believe this is happening to me. SOO Roy Lichtenstein. Like in the *Matrix*. Like, haranguing Gertrude Stein when she pathetically jibed: "Affectations can be dangerous." She's a good writer. I'm alive and celibate. You're fertile. But you loll in my soul like an Adderral, pump in my ribs like stale cigarettes: the self. Yeah, I like you. Poems should not use the word "fuck." Want to read John Ashbery at Steinart Hall?

ॐ

I guess what I intended to impart to you at our last meeting is that I have felt something for you I don't crave, if that means anything -- it does to me. I cannot like what I crave, that is my Catholic curse. I make decisions, declarations of independence, true, but that's the need of these emotions to determine *me* for whatever one might decide my *self* is in the end. Does this make sense? O damn blast my intellect! I'm as happy thinking you are exterior to whatever realistically is my body, but you are also an emanation of it -- of that, I'm quite sure. You trail behind me lightly like scarves, unlike the sashes that dispatched Isadora Duncan ("affectations can be dangerous," Gertrude Stein erroneously let slip) but more ribbons of thought: intent, synaesthetic sorrows, the elixir of memory. You are nearly *heart*, but divorced from it. Poems without torques are the stuff of dissertations, while a poem that turns with carnival festivity is like a "proverbial day of sunshine," as Stefan Gislason wrote to me in an email the other day. The relevance of this to what I am writing now is unclear, but I include it just in case. Emails never use the word "fuck." Do you want to read Berryman with me at Faunce?

I hate the Fibonacci sequence. I tried to tell you this last
time we met. I feel it has nothing to do with you, have *felt*
this for you, if that means anything -- it does to me. I'm a
Catholic curse -- a breast man. Mandelbrot? No. A paucity of
independence? True. But that's the need of these emotions to
determine *me* for whatever one might decide my *fix* is in case
that it matters. It matters. End. Does this make sense? I am
no intellect. I'm as happy thinking you are inside me as I'm
inside your *blah*, get it? You are also an emanation of it --
uh, like a parasite. Uh, not. Duh. You flutter about me like
gaudily-colored scarves in an NY breeze -- "affectations can
be dangerous," Gertrude Stein fatuously harped -- a skein of
delirious, animated hype... my type. You have my heart but I
suck at it. Yeah. Poems are the moss of dissertations, while
poems that turn on Stefan Gislason's proverbial sun... nope.
The relevance of this to what I am writing now is too clear,
but I gloss it just in case. Emails fuck with the brain when
you least expect it, know what I mean? Emails fall like rain
on God in a john when there is nothing to read. I am vetting
my prose for you to weed. Care to analyze Hopkins at Hillel?

℘

Where are you? *You better not be sleeping with an electronic*
writer or I will kick your ass. Fibonacci, Mandelbrot, all a
crock of shit. I tried to tell you this last time we talked.
I feel it has nothing to do with my Catholic curse -- a tits
and ass woman, that's what I am. Talan Memmott? Alan Turing?
No... The need of the emotions to determine *me* for an entire
afternoon, what more does life require? Not AI: certainly in
bed when it matters, this make sense. I am all intellect: as
happy thinking you are nothing but numbers inside me as I am
a barcode rubbing against a government spy satellite. You're
an example of this -- a paragon of sexual script, but a code
nonetheless. Uh, still ill. You flatter me, frankly, kind of
like gaudily-colored scarves in a Providence April breeze --
"affectations can be dangerous," Gertrude Stein once gripped
-- sprites of Flash-animated webby hype... my kind of trite.
You have my heart but I flail at it, for you are fondling it
with your platonic toenails. Uh huh. Poems are often written
for theses though feces often plays its role, as do doctoral
dissertations. Emails by Stefan Gislason... irrelevant, like
what I am writing now. I gloss it for luck: Hopkins is love.

Where are you, now? Driving, parking, now? You better not be
sleeping. I have something to say to you, now. And will kick
your ass if you are sleeping. Fibonacci, Mandelbrot, nothing
for now -- all a hoax. I tried to tell you this last time we
talked. I feel it has something to do with my Christian lust
-- a tits and ass gal, that's what I am. Parasite? No. *Being*
is all I need to determine *me* for an August afternoon, there
is nothing more: life retires. Queerly, this make sense. I'm
no intellect: as happy thinking you are not numbers but text
inside me as I am a poem rubbing against a fireman's crotch.
You're an example of this -- degraded script, poems breathed
into a crowd. Still... contagious. I flatter you, true. This
poem is like an obstinately-patterned scarf in a New England
gust -- "affectations can be dangerous," Gertrude Stein once
toasted -- a voice lashing out against the hype. You are kin
to my light. You own my heart as I disown my past: *stability*
you fondle with your able perspective, keen sight. O fiction
written for an undergrad thesis, be an email now from Stefan
Gislason... smugly irreverent, if terrible luck. I am *raping*
for you to *become*. I'm waiting for you to return my Hopkins.

❧

Who are you? Are you sleeping? I have so many questions, but
you curl next to me like an unsweatered cat: I can only hold
your shoulders, await for you to resurrect. I have some hoax
I hope to reveal: that I've tried, but cannot, *think*. It has
little truck with my suburban prejudices: my lusts -- a tits
and ass man, that's what I am -- pathetic. *Being* that though
not wanting to *be*, for just a single afternoon: life retires
when I sleep next to you, I can barely speak. Strangely, you
make no sense: you sleep. I'm all disease: as happy thinking
you are numbers and text, a weather clouding all my vectors,
my present tense. You're a gospel -- a gilded message -- "X"
marked "contagious" because it violates *me*. This poem is one
such example: scarves in a syntactic breeze -- "affectations
can be dangerous," Gertrude Stein stupidly hinted -- a voice
laughing at my type. You gasp when I bite. You fondle my ass
with your acid trust, your bleeding cut. Fictions written as
serial emails move like worms through a decaying gut, asking
for the check: literate smut. I am retracing these words for
you to arrive between them: I want you to awaken, to become.
I'm waiting for you to *resume*, like Hopkins after his death.

I am out of patience. *When* are you? You have no right to not
be here when I am swamped with criminal misgivings. I do not
have answers, you have questions: we are sorely vexed. I can
only hold your shoulders, wait for you to awaken: our shadow
grave. An *unurban* luxury. The extreme austerity of an almost
empty mind, our only remorse: thinking. That is what I am --
the letters clutter and fall into the bathetic "infinite," a
booby prize for those of us vaguely anxious, "unstable." You
ask me to stop taking my pills, you remark that life retires
when I sleep next to you, you can barely speak: you die. I'm
all cause, but you are no reaction, all obviating rumors and
paralyzed reflexes, an emotional whirlwind that sabotages my
defenses. So I sit, still, my texts "contagious" because all
your diseases are fatal: they choke. This prose for example.
As Gertrude Stein preternaturally averred: "affectations can
be dangerous." She had it right, you shirk at my thesis. You
soil my heart with your toxic distrust: you are greedy for a
butt. Emails I sent to Costa Rica to ask and beg you, careen
like sin through an honest gut. I want these words to *arrive*
you between them. I want them to *writhe*, and free your life.

Second Season: The Island

❧

I wander the island, inventing it. This small, secretive bay
just below what was once the caretaker's cabin. Wrought-iron
poker, grass, the caretaker's son soiling the ruins. A boat,
two girls upon it, coming in off the lake, slowly toward the
shore. One girl standing forward, fashionbook-trim, in tight
gold pants, frowns down over her shoulder at her sister: the
tiny muscles by her ears tense and ripple. The sister, whose
name is Karen (she wears a yellow dress, beige cardigan over
it) remains in the boat as the one in gold pants disembarks.
I guess what I mean to say to you is that I have always felt
that I don't need, or want, to make such choices, even as an
island swims before me, thwarting the idle contexts of these
words: I am happy thinking they are not internal to my body,
my skin, but emanations. Like the scarf that snagged Isadora
Duncan an easy death ("affectations can be dangerous," Stein
quipped) when it got wound in the wheel of her roofless car,
this island drags me deeper into something else: writing. It
is like the proverbial night without stars, revealing a love
for you that is not simply a matter for the meager sovereign
of my island, but brings us further into the verity of text.

I deposit shadows and dampness, spin webs and scatter ruins.
A guest cabin, a porch, a tattered screen door. The girl who
wears gold pants disembarks, watches as the other girl picks
up a yellowish-gray rope from the bottom of the boat, tosses
it to her. A tall slender man, dressed in slacks and a white
turtleneck, leans against a stone parapet smoking a pipe. He
believes he heard a motorboat come to the island. A wrought-
iron poker lies in the grass as the caretaker's son deposits
redolent love letters in the bathrooms: he shits everywhere.
I guess what I want to say to you is: there are antechambers
to everything I want to say to you, and these are them. That
I beg patience as I track this island in correspondence your
imagination might not glean the cruxes of, as letters thwart
the easy commune of these words. I am happy knowing they are
my skin. "Affectations can be dangerous," Gertrude Stein was
heard to have quipped, just as the man, the caretaker, never
trusts what he hears, but *deduces* an aura. A sound drags me:
writing. It is like the proverbial day without rain: my love
for you that is not simply a matter for the meager sovereign
of evening, but casts us deeper toward the aftermath of sex.

❧

I put it there. Has he heard a motorboat come to the island?
The caretaker's son observes their approach through a broken
window of the guest cabin. I put him there. He is stocky and
dark, muscular, hairy, with short, bowed legs. His long hair
slips down his back, his genitals hang thick and heavy below
him and his buttocks are shaggy. I did that. Where are they?
his small eyes seem to ask. The girl in gold pants? Yes. The
other one, Karen? Also. They are sisters. I brought them out
here, as I did the rope, snakes, poker. I put those redolent
love letters in the bathroom: his shit. My work is complete.
I guess what I want to say is: what puts you here puts words
behind you. To say be *you*, these must be them, also. Thus, I
beg patience as I track this poem, like a serial TV show, or
a "Fantasy Island," if you'll forgive a bad pun. Off balance
allusions wend through the blanks between words -- you might
not attain the meaning: blanks thwart meanly a lucid passage
of prose. I am happy knowing nothing, as Gertrude Stein said
it: "Affectations can be dangerous." I put her there: Stein,
the caretaker, the two girls. It's the proverbial *nth* day of
creation but my first birth. I swerve into the path of love.

Squeamishly, she touches it, grips it, picks it up, turns it over. Not so rusty on the underside -- but bugs! *Millions* of them! She drops the thing, shudders, stands, wipes her hands several times on her pants, shudders again. A few steps away she pauses, glances about at everything near her, memorizing the place probably. She hurries up the path, sees her sister already at the first guest cabin. (A guest cabin, a porch, a tattered screen door.) A tall slender man, dressed in slacks and a white turtleneck, leans back and smokes a pipe. He has heard a girl's voice shout "Karen" after a motorboat cut its engine. The caretaker's son limps into the ink dark shadows. I guess what I want to say to you is: there are antechambers to everything. "Affectations can be dangerous," Stein joked, but antechambers have their use, just as chamber pots repose in the shadows of early novels. As the caretaker trusts what he reads, he hears -- what I write never trusts what is said but is his ear's quarry. (A sound drugs me.) What is it that our friend Stefan, infamously, once remarked: a poem without "fuck" is like the proverbial day without sun? Love is never a matter for the eager analyst of the word, if that matters.

⪼

Squeamishly, he touches it, grasps it, picks it up, turns it over. Not so rusty on the underside -- but bugs! *Millions* of them! He drops the thing, shudders, recoils, wipes his hands several times on his pants, recoils again. Many feet away he stumbles, in fact, hurries up the path, sees Karen nearly at the first guest cabin. (A guest cabin with a tattered screen door.) A tall slender woman dressed in tight golden pants, a flouncy blouse, leans backward into the kitchen, but quickly returns. He hears a voice shout "Karen." Is it hers? The son of the caretaker shrinks into the dampened shadows, insanely alert. I guess what I aim to prove is, there are inverses to everything: black turns to white with one sweep of the keys. "Affectations can be dangerous," Stein pouted, but reversals have their uses, just as spaceships doze in the shoulders of hovering Venus. As the caretaker trusts what Karen reads, he hears -- what I write never blames what is written but is an ill ear's verity. (Sound seduces me.) What is it that Stefan -- tall guy with famous hair -- once replied: a poem without "fuck" in it is like the proverbial wine sans bread? Love is not a subject for the seminarian of vision, but lies within.

Squeamishly, she touches it, grips it, picks it up, turns it over. Not so rusty on the underside -- but bugs! *Millions* of them! She kisses the tip -- *poof!* "Thanks," the Knight says, smiling down at her. (The caretaker's son retreats deep into the mottled shade of a bush.) She drops the thing, shudders, stands, wipes her hands several times on her pants, shudders again. She kisses it -- *poof!* Before her appears a tall man, slender, handsome, dressed in dark slacks, white turtleneck, jacket, smoking a pipe. (The caretaker's son, genitals heavy below him, eyes aglitter, slinks into the speckled umbrage.) A motorboat cuts its engine. A girl's voice shouts, "Karen!" What I want to say is: there is a counterpoint to this story we hear, just as product spoils our appreciation of trash or creation our need to destroy. T.S. Eliot wrote: "Poets ought to know as much as will not encroach upon their... necessary laziness." (Frankly amended.) Or as a chamber pot reposes in the shadows of early novels, the caretaker's son seems to be viewing us from the prick of a hero's vantage. "Affectations can be dangerous," Gertrude Stein (frankly repetitive) joked about death, but poems never vulgar are words avoiding life.

⚘

Squeamishly, she touches it, grips it, picks it up, turns it over. She kisses the tip -- *poof!* "Thanks," the Knight says, smiling down at her. A motorboat cuts its engine. The girl's voice shouts, "Karen!" Karen passes deftly through the house as if familiar with it. The girls have gone. "Oh Karen, it's so very sad!" She hears someone call her name. Saxifrage and shinleaf. The caretaker's son squats joyfully above the blue teakettle, depositing... a love letter. "Mmm." She sticks an iron poker between her teeth. "How did you know to kiss it?" he asks. "Call it woman's intuition," she says with a shrug. I never get a chance to say this: there is chaos within this production, for words jut out like kamikaze luddites, intent on thwarting our parsing's slow action -- amply "paratactic" in modern parlance, if deaf to what we call function. "Poets only know what does not encroach upon a necessary laziness," Eliot (sort of) said. The caretaker's son, genitals warting, shrugs. Two girls play "chopsticks" on a green, grand piano. Stein: "Affectations can be dangerous" Gertrude Stein griped about scarves, but poems not at some point pedestrian vulgar are songs void of words Fards. A girl in gold pants -- comas

The bay once possessed its own system of docks, built out to protect boats from the rocks along the shore. Silver fish as thin as fingernails fog the bottom. Bedded deep in the grass near the path to the first guest cabin lies the wrought-iron poker, long, slender, with an intricately worked handle. The rust that clings to it is a warm orange. The main house is a mansion from which extends a kind of veranda or terrace high out on the promontory giving a spectacular view of the lake. The mansion has many rooms cluttered with debris. Fireplaces and a musty basement, wasps' nests, a grand hexagonal loggia and bright red doors. A green grand piano, its wires pulled. I never get a chance to see quite as clearly as I do now the frame of our geography, for syllables joust, projectiles, or reek in their corners, dismaying us. Like kamikaze luddites, we charge through the glass beyond intention, frankly, or *on* something, yet hardly emoting. Intent on warping being's dim action, poets are lazy. Two poets play "chopsticks" on grand pianos but can't screw in a light bulb. Stein: "Affectations can be dangerous," but of other things she did not tell. Old songs are idle echoes, like anthems penned on a desert isle.

&

"Karen!" the girl in pants calls from outside. (She has just kissed the iron poker?) She bounds up over the rotted second step of the porch and opens the screen door. Karen, about to enter the kitchen (where she saw the caretaker's son?) turns back, smiling. "Karen, I -- oh, *good God!*" (She's discovered the gifts of the caretaker's son? No.) "Judas God!" (Now she has.) She shrieks: "About a hundred million people have gone to the *bathroom* in there!" (Earlier, did she not gush: "They even had *electricity*"?) And do they see a green grand piano? I think (intent on warping being's thin fiction?) I am next. I am next to your body now, waiting for you to call. (Others are simple who, vulgar, merely talk.) One can't screw in the dark so we play on pianos or doze in the shadows of credible novellas. (Of other things, did she not tell?) "Affectations can be dangerous" I seem to remember (did I not ever know?), as was once said by a writer who recoiled from fact. (I suck at remembering: was it *her* intention?) Planning to dissemble I retain very little, like the genital's son whose cares are unknowing. What I want to say is: I'm a fount of forgetting. In service stairs the sweet corruption thrives, a poet sang.

In service stairs the sweet corruption thrives, a poet sang. *Someone goes around the rooms and drives his fists into each wall, shatters every window, because he wants to hurt. Where have all the princes gone? But it isn't those who pine after things they want or need or even don't need and take them as they please, it's the people who destroy, destroy because... lust! That's all, Karen! And they've pulled the strings from the grand green piano! And then they went to the bathroom on it all! It's a sad place. Sad, and yet all too right for me, I suppose.* (The girl in gold pants is waxing philosophical.) *What I mean to say is, I'm so miserable. And yet sometimes I believe that I can draw. Call it an odd, semi-precious urge. I am simple and vulgar -- just look at my golden pants, from which I have hoped for years to be disinterred. An author or prince, a knight or comedian, might come who could fidget my slim legs from within them. I want to draw him* (but he's not on the island) *or free him from the cell of a magic wrought- iron poker* (yes, he *is* the object). *It might make me seem an undefined woman, and "affectations can be dangerous," I seem to remember. But it's something I want to do, so I'll do it.*

✍

I guess what I am trying to say to you is that I've designed an island: you are now on it. I've put there a faltering old mansion, a goon who walks around without his pants on, a few objects with curious Freudian resonances (a snake, a spider, not to mention a wrought-iron poker) and a tall, slender, if a bit smarmy man who wears a turtleneck sweater, jacket, and smokes pipes (and resembles not a little porn publisher Hugh Hefner circa 1969, the year that I was born in). "In service stairs the sweet corruption thrives," the poet Ashbery wrote (iambic pentameter) in his poem "Pyrography." I am attracted to you as I am to the girl with gold pants, that is obvious. I am attracted to the fly in the sun and to the laughter you animate the smarmy man in the turtleneck with as he is being drawn, depicted as he is a stocky moron who refuses to honor his drawers. This I am trying to impress upon you: to love's to err, and in error we are one, though the future, thus, is not so much a moving forward as moving through, like scarves tossed in the breeze, joint boredoms simultaneously (as Ezra Pound once wrote) "exquisite and excessive." So speak to me. ("Affectations can be dangerous," as Stein once prophesied.)

Once upon a time there was a beautiful young Princess who in tight gold pants made the author of novels and poems write a fairy tale instead that involved a dashing if not very smart Knight and a hirsute if somewhat clever, lustful Caretaker's Son who steals the Magic Poker which he could do because his father's connections were strong and shows up on the day the tournament for the Princess takes place and so he points the Magic Poker at her golden haunches saying *voila* so the pants fall in a puddle on the floor while the Princess rebounds by kissing the Magic Poker producing a Knight in gleaming white and navy blue armor smoking a pipe who smites with his sword the runt of a suitor but a wee bit too soon for she is now a widow (this Princess of the kingdom) as she married the runt the moment she was freed. I guess what I mean to say is that my body is just one manifestation of what I feel for you the other makes sense only in story something manifold with many voices clinging to its coil weaving in and out brightly like scarves rolling you inside them though finally not too ready for the revelation of your words and the body that you offer once you lunge from behind them oh my spurious affectations!

Third Season: Harold and Sonia

୨

How can anybody dislike *cheese?* If you don't mind my pushing this question further: does sanity yet exist in New England, in Little Belknap's head for example, he who deigns not take his cheese even with his spaghetti (the two *do* go together), he who, without a touch of foreign blood, yet manages a curb on all the subtle decencies, those on which I depend and can barely survive without: cheese, cheese and more *cheese!* Hate Roquefort, dislike cottage cheese, rarely tolerate Camembert and Brie, and am neutral about Limburger (this last of which I've only tried once at Whitehead's a year ago this spring). I guess what I mean to write presently is: cheese. That made by Kraft -- the common, vulgar variety -- I have always felt I want, or need when I cannot make purer choices, when Rhode Island rises before me, retarding the ample gravity of these words. I am happy thinking cheese is internal to my body, my skin, my emanations, like the scarves that caught the dancer Isadora, compelling her to an early death ("affectations can be dangerous," the poetaster Stein humorlessly parried) when it tangled in the spokes of a horseless carriage. Providence drags *me* deeper into writing, but it's cheese I lately love.

Sonia, I am writing this under an appreciable mental strain, since by tonight I shall be no more. My supply of the "drug" which alone makes my life endurable, cheese... I'm joking of course, seeking to cheer you up in your subpar city. But how (again) can anybody dislike *cheese?* Little Belknap, that odd fellow, was by here again today and was recalcitrant. We are very much in agreement on other things -- beans for example. Not many doors away, on the other side of Willoughby St., is a restaurant that specializes in home-baked beans. A serving of beans is fifteen cents, with pork, twenty cents. Belknap, without a touch of foreign blood, and who can enjoy a potato in fried form and Postum, nonetheless remains this figure of the tyro when concerning the fine decencies: cheese, cheese, and more *cheese.* What I mean to write to you is: New England is mine, and it owes me a living, and the idea of you in New York with migrant cretins is driving me insane. Affectations can be dangerous, this I know heartily, so I do not write in order to inflate undue desire for my presence. You engage me deeper into my writing -- the Dagon swims before me, fish of hate. Though it's cheese I love, it's you that I am craving.

∿

I am writing this since I may not write again, as by tonight I shall be no more. Ampoules of that which alone is a mind's balm, my sense of self... I'm joking, no *self* reveals itself at any time of my writing, and that's a relief. I am brashly trying to enliven your mind with my thoughts on life, as how (again) can anybody dislike *health?* Little Belknap, a dwarf, but with a normal-sized skull, is no paragon. Of vegetables, I like peas and onions, can tolerate cabbage and turnips, am neutral toward cauliflower, and have no deep enmity toward a carrot, will dodge parsnips and asparagus, shun string beans and Brussels sprout and venomously abominate spinach. I like rhubarb... Belknap, with a drop of Asian blood, likes Postum but recoils at these opinions. Why bother? "Affectations can be dangerous," as Gertrude Stein, the expat's expat, loopily expressed, and though New England is blind and blows me off, New York with its miscreant hordes only lures the white race into miscegenation and passivity. This I believe heartily: I write to instigate an appetite within me for your scent. You drag me deep into story, as the Dagon masticates on humanity before me. Let me lure you to fate, though the ruse be love.

I'm writing: Hershey's sweet chocolate is one of my favorite nibbles. I'm drifting aimlessly beneath a scorching sun. I'm no more, in nearly any form. Vials of that which alone is my heart's tomb, my soul's menace... I'm joking, you know: coco is not so much my disease (unlike cheese) though it provides a relief from this black tension. I'm merely trying to angle my imagination with these notes on health, as how can anyone frankly disregard *fruit?* What an unsubtle condition, what an attitudinal *faux pas*, what a mental divorce! Little Belknap, himself a joke, but with a nominal investment in the *normal,* recalled: he likes peas and onions, cannot humor cabbage and turnips, is neutral toward cauliflower, but doesn't tolerate parsnips and asparagus at all, which (in *that* case) is as it should be. With a drop of Indian blood, Belknap likes bagels and Postum, but recoils at jellies and jams. What do I mean? What was it that Christopher Smart said: Affectations can be dangerous? Or was that Stein, the Jew? Though New England is lurid and it snows in July, New York with its mixing minions only divides the white race between the haves and have-nots, and I'm thirty-four with no job skill. Am I too old to love?

᪾

Sonia... Sonia... Sonia... you are great. But, as for jam or jelly, I am your utter opposite, for I enjoy it so well that I pile on amounts thicker than the bread that sustains them! Only joking. I'm drifting aimlessly beneath a scorching sun. I'm no more. I am coursing and free. Capsules of whatever it is that is my bastard being's substance (unlike cheese) does not do me justice, perverts my sexuality with these notes on love, as how can anyone frankly disregard *bed?* What a tragic condition, what an attitudinal *je ne sais quas*, what a venal hoarse call! Little Belknap, he the poet and dissembler, but with a nominal investment in the *army*, said: he prefers peas and scallions, cannot stomach salmon and pike, is ambivalent toward broccoli and masculine destiny, but can't provide the time of day to beets and celery, as (in this latter case) is cool, primarily. He has a drop of Spanish blood but requests lattes and Postum, and recoils at cappuccinos and espressos. I mean... what? What was it Ashbery wrote: "Affectations can be dangerous?" Or was that a young Stein, yet to pen novels? Though England dreams, New York with its colored proletariat keeps me awake with its nightmare of equality. Oh democracy.

Sonia... Sonia... Sonia... the change happened while I read.
There was very little I could do: you are great. As for jam,
jelly or cheese, I am your utter slave, for I enjoy what you
write so well, I pile on slabs of my being immenser than the
page you bred (breed). That sustains me! I'm not joking. I'm
drifting breathlessly beneath a cappuccino sun (no kidding),
I'm no more than a course without fee (it's near the truth).
Pills of whatever I take as my special psychotherapy (unlike
virgins in tow) can do me justice, corrupts my homosexuality
with pregnant notes from above, as how can anyone accurately
canonize *text?* What a comic condition! What a Borgesian, uh,
whatever. What a viral Morse code! Tiny Belknap, he the born
tin prophet, but with a tendency toward *photography,* farted:
he prefers peas and scallions, hates Scandinavian Benedicts,
is ambivalent toward girls and boys, but can't agree the sun
acts upon the sea, the time of day on leeks and parsley, for
(in this first case) the moon has a *disease.* He has a splash
of Croatian blood (he vomits with an accent) but digs lattes
and Bloody Marys, like a fey ray. I say: lame. "Affectations
can be dangerous"? (Stein?) Or: nightmare on Decency Street.

%

I saw protruding from the nasty mud an unending pain. Sonia,
the changes happened in bed. On the third morning I saw soil
dry enough to walk upon with ease. There was nothing I could
do: you *are,* again. As for ice cream, my favorite tastes are
vanilla and coffee (the latter difficult to find outside New
England), and my least relished common flavor is strawberry.
You are my one salve: I have said that the unbroken monotony
of the rolling plain was a source of vague horror to me, for
I enjoy how you deign to castigate me, to aim insult into my
abdomen. That sustains me! I'm not drifting, but I'm not the
same: a voice flung. Breathlessly under a modicum of sun (no
kidding), I'm coursing, panting, sweating. Whatever I imbibe
as my paltry pharmacology (like viruses in pills) affects me
nichts, affirms my duality with random piano notes like that
idiot John Cage. How can anyone truly gamble talents? What a
cosmic retaliation! Belknap, never good at pontificating (he
has a big head) prefers scotch and olives, pursues girls and
boys, but can't see the word martyrs sex. He has a splash of
foreign blood, denies the basic decencies: "Affectations can
be dangerous" (G. Stein). The neighbors think I'm atrocious.

Protruding from the mud: a plinth. The script was a language of hieroglyphics unknown to me and unlike anything ever seen in books, consisting largely of conventional aquatic symbols such as fishes, eels, octopi, crustaceans, molluscs, sharks, whales and the like. Sonia, I'm not kidding: the woof warped in bed. Grotesque beyond the imagination of a Poe or Bulwer, they were damnably human in outline despite webbed hands and feet, shockingly wide and flabby lips, glassy, bulging eyes, and other features less pleasant to recall. Sonia, the swill swellt timely. On the third morning I found soil hard enough to trek upon. There was something: *myself.* Vast, Polyphemus-like, and loathsome, it darted like a creature of nightmares to the monolith, about which it flung its huge, moist, scaly arms, the while it bowed its hideous head and gave vent to a stereograph of certain measured sounds. "Affectations can be dangerous" moaned a plangent G. Stein, and Belknap, being an Albanian American, confirms my guilt with fanciful falsetto. I cannot think of the deep sea without shame at the nameless things that at this very moment are crawling, floundering on its warm, phlegmatic bed. Thus, my preference for ice cream.

֍

Dear Howard: oh, how my artichoke heart quakes -- but that's not what I mean. What I mean to write is... useless. I am no pen to your Poe-brain. Nothing is obvious, but lentils, when properly paired, provide its diners amino acid extravaganza. Howard, I'm serious: my tender buttons wilt in your stead, I am at a loss at how to cool down. Fearing food is unfounded, perhaps little Belknap has yet to fork the choicest cheeses? The fairest fromage? As for glassy, bulging eyes and similar outward features: New York is mine, and it owes me a living, but I haven't sold a hat in four weeks and will have to shut the millinery. "Affectations can be dangerous" said a gadfly (E. Nesbit?) but she obviously knew nothing of Fashion Week. Splendid suppers necessitate depth, and depth isn't realized but in the deepest reds... But red was last spring. My sweet Howard! (Let me start again.) What I mean to say is: dessert completes a meal. I allow myself a small dessert once a week (for I want to stay, as they say, petit -- the French have a way with worries). Send me your latest weird stories, but no more grief about immigrants: some of my best fish are Greek. And, although it is beets I crave, the best soups are green.

Sonia... Sonia... Sonia... thanks for the cheese (which I'll not eat, because it's Greek) and thanks for the letter which I'll reread for the next week (until the cheese doth wilt in my heart, which is weak). Fond of sausage -- most especially the old fashioned baked or fried sort. Like fowl -- but only the white meat. Dark meat I can't bear, but I think you know that already (and I'm not talking about immigrants, green or yellow or Lebanese, much as it freeze my liberalism). Really favourite meal is the regular old New England turkey dinner, with highly seasoned dressing, cranberry sauce, onions, etc. and mince pie for dessert. Yum. (Did I just type "Yum"?) Let me start again... I wander Rhode Island, inventing it (after all, I *am* Providence), find poetry in the common, vulgar way neighborhoods shoot up, procreate, or decay. You say it's my Poe-brain -- it is really a love for the horror of life, how it plies my gut... into writing. I'm writing to say plainly: this is my love for you, you make a Spring of me, and though "Affectations can be dangerous," as Gertrude Stein says, you must understand me: I don't despise the Greeks, but the Cape Verdian population makes me crazy. And you are Sonia Greene.

&

Sonia... Sonia... Sonia... thanks for the cheese (which I'll eat, because you are Sonia Greene) and thanks for the letter which I have read many times this week, in Greek, Ukrainian, French, and, yes, Portuguese. I've even read it in Jewish (I am a completist.) However, still fond of sausage. One cannot change one's stripes. Yummy. (Did I just type "Yummy," too?) Let me start again... I wander the island, inventing it -- I *am* Providence, and find poetry in the coarse, aching way the neighbors ask me for money. You say it's my Defoe-brain -- I am nothing of an islander if I am not *imaginatively* alone, a lantern-jawed, Edwardian Crusoe. Maybe, maybe. "Affectations can be dangerous" I'm well aware (yes, that's Stein), but it is also an addiction to the high horrors of life that emerge only in a pristine solitude, a type that is rare, found only in the bleeding of history into rot that is New England. I'm even beginning to like Cape Verdians, and the tattooed sorts that stumble down Empire Street can almost make me desecrate my celibacy. (I am kidding.) I am writing to write floridly: you are my crisis, my one, and hence, my dilemma: you make a Spring of all, and I've a sun of mud. So, let's get married.

I guess what I mean to say to you is that I have always felt
that I don't need, or want, to make the decisions in my life
but rather that I need *deep hungers* to determine them for me
whatever one might decide "hunger" is in the end. I have, as
is my predilection, often compared them to slimy fish, or to
alien, ghastly creatures that have inundated my sensibility,
humiliated my consciousness, and rendered towns and villages
hells of mindful corpses. As our friend Stefan Gislason (not
one of the dead) succinctly wrote: "a poem without 'fuck' in
it is like the proverbial day without sunshine" (yes, he's a
mensch). But I'm not joking: I like Cape Verdians, and being
with you in New York, while brief and trying, was cloud nine
for *this* mensch (who is dying). Sonia, a cancer has breached
my throat. My affectations, never wholly safe, have betrayed
me to dangers. I'm an artist without a net, and now, without
you, have barely enough to eat: anxiety snares, rats claw at
my intestines, I have paralyzing dreams. I made seventy-five
cents on my latest story, and though I'm being paid to edit,
carpal tunnel slays my wrists, and I have little to cash but
cliché. I love you, Sonia Greene. Til we meet in the Cave...

Two Introductory Essays

֍

I. What Is Electronic Writing?

I'm asked this question quite often, and have rarely been able to come up with a short answer. It's many things, and quite often, a work of "electronic writing" is so unique that it's a genre until itself.

If I were to come up with a fortune cookie answer to the question, I would say that it is any form of writing that takes advantage of the possibilities afforded by digital technology—such as the internet, or graphics programs such as Illustrator or Photoshop, or animation /audio /interactive programs such as Flash—in their creation and presentation.

But it is also those forms of writing that are informed by new ways of thinking brought on by the way digital technology has impacted our world, i.e. forms of writing that are organized according to the principles of the database, or that work primarily as texts distributed over the internet, or that—in the manner of "Dispositions," which was written with the aid of a GPS device—relied on computer technology in the writing.

Now for the long answer... electronic writing can be:

- **Classic hypertext fiction,** in which different pages of writing (often called "lexia") are maneuvered by the reader by clicking on words or images. These can be "choose your own adventure" type narratives, or more poetic interactive texts in which there are no fictional elements at all. Many of the better ones of these, such as "Patchwork Girl" and "Afternoon," are not available online, and have to be purchased from Eastgate Systems. Online texts include works by Talan Memmott, Geoff Ryman, Claire Dinsmore, Yael Kanarek, Stephanie Strickland and Stuart Moulthrop, along with freebies at the Eastgate reading room.
- **Animated poems,** such as "The Dreamlife of Letters" or "Axolotl," in which the viewer/reader is not asked to do anything but watch and listen while text performs before them. Think of this as the art of movie titles applied to creative ventures. "Bembo's Zoo" is another classic example, and the Flash movies of "Young-Hae Chang Heavy Industries" (and possibly "JibJab") are distant cousins.
- **Conceptual blogs and websites,** such as "The Dullest Blog in the World" or "Dagmar Chili Pitas," which are sites that explore a particular type of writing to the nth degree, such that you really can't categorize them under anything in particular. "Entropy8," by Aurelia Harvey, is a classic in this genre.
- **Non-electronic conceptual writing,** such as "The Tapeworm Foundry" or "Dispositions," that explore some aspect of writing that relates to a "database aesthetic," i.e. a collection of fragments that are organized in a mathematic or otherwise highly systematic

(non-lyrical and non-narrative) way. Process or "uncreative" writing, such as Kenneth Goldsmith's "No. 111," is another example of this.

- **Parody and "hactivist" websites**, which are conceptual sites that attempt to comment on the conventions of public communication on the web, such as "whitehouse.org," my own "Vaneigem Series," or "Blackness for Sale," which was really just a page of Ebay. These sites usually engage in some form of artistic plagiarism, i.e. taking graphics and design elements from mainstream sites and detourning them.
- **Wordtoys**, which are more sophisticated forms of classic hypertext, in which the user is invited to play with an experimental interface in such a way that new textual creations are manufactured in real-time, such as Camille Utterback's installation "Text Rain" or the projects of Daniel Howe. Experimental interfaces such as on the "Eclipse" website or the "Visual Thesaurus" are a version of this.
- **Interactive Fiction and literary games**, in which the user is the hero of a story, and must input commands to navigate the literary piece and solve it like a puzzle, in the manner of early text-playing or role-playing games. Nick Montfort has been the biggest advocate of this type of writing.
- **Cave Writing and installation texts**, which takes place in the virtual reality environment of Brown's Cave or in galleries, like "Text Rain" or "Legible City." Some installations, such as work by Jenny Holzer or Mark Domino's "glås," are not interactive.
- **Email and collaborative art** and other forms of writing that take advantage of the forms of communication peculiar to electronic media—such as "Implementation," which is a fiction that requires the user to download stickers that they can paste up in the cities or towns they live in—or even writing that is primarily distributed via text messaging.
- **Computer generated texts**, in which a computer program helped in the creation of the text, or in which a web spider culled live text from the internet to create the work, such as in Noah Wardrip-Fruin's "Regime Change" and "Newsreader." A version of this is website translators like "Pornolize.com," which converts the text of any website into a (kitschy) porn language.
- **Documentary websites**—such as ubu.com, a collection of concrete, audio and avant-garde video files, and rhizome.org, the premiere internet website—are often considered a form of art since they are often the expressions of very personal, non-commercial and even obsessive artistic and political visions and often create distinct communities of users. William Poundstone's electronic essay "New Digital Emblems" is a great example of a website that is both beautiful and informative.

There are a billion variations on the above, and in fact no piece is ever peculiar to one of these categories. A work called "They Rule," which is fed by a database of CEOs of the major corporations of the world, is an interactive political cartoon that is almost entirely a textual experience, while "All Your Base Are Belong to Us" is just a crazy Flash movie made by any number of people spontaneously around the world.

Great electronic art can be created with little or no computer skills, which is kind of the drama of the entire venture. Some of the most effective forms of electronic writing are INCREDIBLY SIMPLE to create, such as "Blackness for Sale" and the "Vaneigem Series." I have a soft spot for these types of projects, since they don't require a team of computer scientists, and their impact is clean and immediate.

II. Themes and Concepts

Keep in mind that very little is entirely "new" in "new media writing." There are often examples from the analog world that explain certain principles of electronic writing even better than the electronic writing available.

Some of the following terminology might sound INCREDIBLY PRETENTIOUS. At least I think it does, but I also think these concepts are pretty handy to keep in mind when reading (and playing) the work assigned for this semester. They are not concepts you would be dealing with too often in other art or literature classes.

Recombinant poetics is the aesthetics of treating words and letters like digital objects. "Collage poetics," like what the Dada and Surrealist artists explored in their games, or "cut up" methods explored by William S. Burroughs, treated words like physical objects, and used chance to create new combinations that were startling to the reader and not governed by an "author." Oulipo writing practices, in which formulas were used as constraints on the writing—a simple one being the non-use of the letter "e" in George Perec's novel *A Void*—treated language as something mathematical, almost like numbers, though never to the degree of being illegible.

"Recombinant poetics" is something like both of these, but in the digital realm, hence opening the possibilities of 1) employing incredibly complex writing algorithms, and 2) accessing a possibly infinite world of texts, either through the internet or one's own files. John Cayley has probably written the most on this subject in relation to his own work in "text morphing."

The above is closely related to something I call **database aesthetics**, which is a phrase that I accidentally stole from the critic and theorist Lev Manovich. Works predicated on a database aesthetics explore organizing texts in ways that haven't arisen in literary history in the genres we are familiar with (poetry, drama, and fiction) but rather have arisen through our working with databases, sorting alphabetically, by length, by occurrence of certain elements, by keywords, etc. Works like Lyn Hejinian's poem *My Life*, which, in the version she wrote when she was 37, had 37 chapters of 37 sentences each, is a precursor of this.

Text/image complex are those moments when the text and image of a piece (or even the image of text itself) interact in a way that moves beyond illustration, and beyond what either element is doing on its own. A good, basic example of this is your standard New Yorker cartoon—neither the drawing or the caption are very funny on their own, but the caption makes you see something different in the drawing, or vice versa. Advertisements play on this principle quite often—the phrase "Think different." attached to a picture of Mahatma Gandhi creates a little "a ha" moment in the brain, much like when reading a haiku.

There can also be a sound element, but since we won't be dealing with sound in this class, it's better to keep in mind the use of text/image in works. The image of a text comes into play in works such as the books of Kenneth Goldsmith, which are predicated on giving physical mass to collections of words, or in pieces such as "Cedars Estate," where the words are design elements. The text/image complex usually has some element of paradox or contradiction to it; the text and image are working against each other as much as for.

I also occasionally use the phrase **visual pun**. By that, I mean any instance in which the visual image appears to be one thing, but then, after the application of a caption, or maybe with a "pullback," as in a movie, the image is revealed to be something quite different than what you thought it was. William Poundstone's "New Media Emblems" are examples of visual puns, as are "Bembo's Zoo" and the New Yorker Cartoons. Another well-known example is that gestalt game where you think you are either looking at an old hag or a young woman, though this might be classed more as an optical illusion.

The **interface** of a piece is pretty easy to describe: it is the way the piece functions as something you operate. The dashboard of a car is an interface, and even a book—its cover, the binding, the size—is an interface. All websites have an interface, and some incredibly simple interfaces, like that for Google, or ugly interfaces, like that for craigslist, have been the most successful on the web. Many works of electronic writing have experimental interfaces that have to be learned and practiced a little before the piece is truly enjoyable. Others simply have terrible interfaces. Edward Tufte has been the most adamant in his approach to interface reform, especially regarding Power Point.

Generative art and **generative text** are pieces in which the visual or textual image are created live, in real-time, either with the influence of a user's input—moving the mouse around the screen, typing keywords in, etc.—or simply create themselves on their own, in ways determined by an algorithm, usually with some random elements.

The visual pieces of "dextro.org" are beautiful examples of generative art that almost look like highly complex, abstract pencil sketches, while "News Reader" and "Regime Change" are pieces that generate new texts from internet news sources. In these pieces, the artistry is often contained entirely in the programming, though of course none of these pieces can be deemed successful unless the output of the work is pleasurable, perhaps a match for human, non-computer creativity. (There is also something called generative music, which is actually the oldest of the three; Brian Eno was a big advocate of this.)

LINKS AND REFERENCES

The following list is limited to those projects mentioned in the previous essays and is not meant to be an exhaustive survey of electronic writing. All were active (with the exception of the Eclipse site) as of May 28, 2006.

"All Your Base Are Belong to Us." Flash video. <http://rmitz.org/AYB3.swf>

Cave Writing. Documentation of Cave works. <http://www.cascv.brown.edu/cavewriting>

Cayley, John. Artist homepage with links to works. <http://www.shadoof.net>

De Vicq de Cumptich , Roberto. *Bembo's Zoo*. Web-version of children's book.
    <http://www.bemboszoo.com>

Dextro.org. Main site of art project. <http://www.dextro.org>

Dinsmore, Claire. Homepage with links to works. <http://www.studiocleo.com>

Domino, Mark. "glǎs." Documentation of gallery project.
    <http://www.fieldform.com/project.php?id=3>

Eclipse. Web-based art archive, now defunct. <http://www.princeton.edu/eclipse>

Fitterman, Rob and Rowntree, Dirk. "Cedars Estate." Main site of art project.
    <http://www.ubu.com/contemp/rown/cedars/cedars01.html>

Goldsmith, Kenneth. EPC homepage with links to works.
    <http://epc.buffalo.edu/authors/goldsmith>

Harvey, Aurelia. *Entropy8*. Web-based art-project. <http://www.entropy8.com/index2.html>

Hobogrammathon, Toadex. *Dagmar Chili Pitas*. Experimental blog. <http://dagmar_chili.pitas.com>

Howe, Daniel. Homepage with links to works. <http://mrl.nyu.edu/~dhowe/etext.html>

Jackson, Shelley. *Patchwork Girl*. Book published by Eastgate Systems.
    <http://www.eastgate.com/catalog/PatchworkGirl.html>

JibJab. Main site of artist group, links to works. <http://jibjab.com>

Joyce, Michael. *Afternoon*. Hypertext published by Eastgate Systems.
    <http://www.eastgate.com/catalog/Afternoon.html>

Kanarek, Yael. *World of Awe*. Web-based hypertext. <http://worldofawe.net/index.html>

Lopez, Lyndon Cordero. "Axolotl." Web-based animated poem.
    <http://www.arras.net/brown_ewriting/wp-content/uploads/2006/01/axolotl.html>

Manovich, Lev. Main site of theorist with links to essays. <http://www.manovich.net>

Memmott, Talan. Homepage with links to works. <http://memmott.org/talan>

Montfort, Nick and Rettberg, Scott. Implementation. Main site of art project.
    <http://nickm.com/implementation>

Montfort, Nick. Artist main site with information on interactive fiction. <http://nickm.com/if>

Moulthrop, Stuart. Homepage with links to works. <http://iat.ubalt.edu/moulthrop/hypertexts>

New Yorker Cartoons Caption Contest. <http://www.newyorker.com/captioncontest>

Obadike, Keith. "Blackness for Sale." Web-based art project. <http://obadike.tripod.com/ebay.html>

Old Hag or Young Woman. Just so you know what she looks like.
    <http://www.beyondtheveil.net/images/woman.gif>

On, Josh. *They Rule*. Main site of art project. <http://www.theyrule.net>

Pornolize.com. Main site of art project. <http://nickm.com/implementation>

Poundstone, William. "New Digital Emblems" and other works.
        <http://www.williampoundstone.net>

Rhizome.org. Main site of organization. <http://rhizome.org>

Ryman, Geoff. Web version of novel *341*. <http://www.ryman-novel.com>

Shaw, Jeffrey. *Legible City*. Documentation of gallery project. <http://www.jeffrey-
        shaw.net/html_main/frameset-works.php3>

Stefans, Brian Kim. "The Dreamlife of Letters." Web-based animated poem.
        <http://www.arras.net/RNG/flash/dreamlife/dreamlife_index.html>

Stefans, Brian Kim. "Vaneigem Series." Web-based art project. <http://www.whitehouse.org>

Strickland, Stephanie. Homepage with links to works. <http://www.stephaniestrickland.com>

The Dullest Blog in the World. Experimental blog. <http://www.wibsite.com/wiblog/dull>

Tufte, Edward. Main site of theorist with book ordering info. <http://www.edwardtufte.com/tufte>

Ubu.com. Main site of sound, video, concrete poetry archive. <http://www.ubu.com/ubu>

Utterbeck, Camille and Achituv, Romy. "Text Rain." Documentation of gallery project.
        <http://www.camilleutterback.com/textrain.html>

Visual Thesaurus. Web-based thesaurus. <http://www.visualthesaurus.com/?vt>

Wardrip-Fruin and Durand, David. "Regime Change" and "Newsreader." Generative hypertext.
        <http://turbulence.org/Works/twotxt/index.htm>

Wark, McKenzie. *Dispositions*. Book published by Salt Publishing.
        <http://www.saltpublishing.com/books/smf/1876857250.htm>

Wershler-Henry, Darren. *The Tapeworm Foundry*. Web-version of book.
        <http://www.ubu.com/ubu/wershler_tapeworm.html>

Whitehouse.org. Main site of artist group. <http://www.whitehouse.org>

Young-Hae Chang Heavy Industries. Main site of artist group, links to works.
        <http://www.yhchang.com>

ROOF BOOKS

☐ Andrews, Bruce. **Co**. Collaborations with Barbara Cole, Jesse Freeman, Jessica Grim, Yedda Morrison, Kim Rosefield. 104p. $12.95.

☐ Andrews, Bruce. **Ex Why Zee**. 112p. $10.95.

☐ Andrews, Bruce. **Getting Ready To Have Been Frightened**. 116p. $7.50.

☐ Benson, Steve. **Blue Book**. Copub. with The Figures. 250p. $12.50

☐ Bernstein, Charles. **Controlling Interests**. 80p. $11.95.

☐ Bernstein, Charles. **Islets/Irritations**. 112p. $9.95.

☐ Bernstein, Charles (editor). **The Politics of Poetic Form**. 246p. $12.95; cloth $21.95.

☐ Brossard, Nicole. **Picture Theory**. 188p. $11.95.

☐ Cadiot, Olivier. **Former, Future, Fugitive**. Translated by Cole Swensen. 166p. $13.95.

☐ Champion, Miles. **Three Bell Zero**. 72p. $10.95.

☐ Child, Abigail. **Scatter Matrix**. 79p. $9.95.

☐ Davies, Alan. **Active 24 Hours**. 100p. $5.

☐ Davies, Alan. **Signage**. 184p. $11.

☐ Davies, Alan. **Rave**. 64p. $7.95.

☐ Day, Jean. **A Young Recruit**. 58p. $6.

☐ Di Palma, Ray. **Motion of the Cypher**. 112p. $10.95.

☐ Di Palma, Ray. **Raik**. 100p. $9.95.

☐ Doris, Stacy. **Kildare**. 104p. $9.95.

☐ Doris, Stacy. **Cheerleader's Guide to the World: Council Book** 88p. $12.95.

☐ Dreyer, Lynne. **The White Museum**. 80p. $6.

☐ Dworkin, Craig. **Strand**. 112p. $12.95.

☐ Edwards, Ken. **Good Science**. 80p. $9.95.

☐ Eigner, Larry. **Areas Lights Heights**. 182p. $12, $22 (cloth).

☐ Gardner, Drew. **Petroleum Hat**. 96p. $12.95.

☐ Gizzi, Michael. **Continental Harmonies**. 96p. $8.95.

☐ Gladman, Renee. **A Picture-Feeling**. 72p. $10.95.

☐ Goldman, Judith. **Vocoder**. 96p. $11.95.

☐ Gottlieb, Michael. **Ninety-Six Tears**. 88p. $5.

☐ Gottlieb, Michael. **Gorgeous Plunge**. 96p. $11.95.

☐ Gottlieb, Michael. **Lost & Found**. 80p. $11.95.

☐ Greenwald, Ted. **Jumping the Line**. 120p. $12.95.

☐ Grenier, Robert. **A Day at the Beach**. 80p. $6.

☐ Grosman, Ernesto. **The XULReader: An Anthology of Argentine Poetry (1981–1996)**. 167p. $14.95.

☐ Guest, Barbara. **Dürer in the Window, Reflexions on Art**. Book design by Richard Tuttle. Four color throughout. 80p. $24.95.

☐ Hills, Henry. **Making Money**. 72p. $7.50. VHS videotape $24.95. Book & tape $29.95.

☐ Huang Yunte. **SHI: A Radical Reading of Chinese Poetry**. 76p. $9.95

☐ Hunt, Erica. **Local History**. 80 p. $9.95.

☐ Kuszai, Joel (editor) **poetics@**, 192 p. $13.95.

☐ Inman, P. **Criss Cross**. 64 p. $7.95.

☐ Inman, P. **Red Shift**. 64p. $6.

☐ Lazer, Hank. **Doublespace**. 192 p. $12.

☐ Levy, Andrew. **Paper Head Last Lyrics**. 112 p. $11.95.

☐ Mac Low, Jackson. **Representative Works: 1938–1985**. 360p. $18.95 (cloth).

☐ Mac Low, Jackson. **Twenties**. 112p. $8.95.

☐ McMorris, Mark. **The Café at Light**. 112p. $12.95.

□ Moriarty, Laura. **Rondeaux**. 107p. $8.
□ Neilson, Melanie. **Civil Noir**. 96p. $8.95.
□ Osman, Jena. **An Essay in Asterisks**. 112p. $12.95.
□ Pearson, Ted. **Planetary Gear**. 72p. $8.95.
□ Perelman, Bob. **Virtual Reality**. 80p. $9.95.
□ Perelman, Bob. **The Future of Memory**. 120p. $14.95.
□ Perelman, Bob. **IFLIFE**. 136p. $13.95.
□ Piombino, Nick, **The Boundary of Blur**. 128p. $13.95.
□ Prize Budget for Boys, **The Spectacular Vernacular Revue**. 96p. $14.95.
□ Raworth, Tom. **Clean & Will-Lit**. 106p. $10.95.
□ Robinson, Kit. **Balance Sheet**. 112p. $11.95.
□ Robinson, Kit. **Democracy Boulevard**. 104p. $9.95.
□ Robinson, Kit. **Ice Cubes**. 96p. $6.
□ Rosenfield, Kim. **Good Morning—MIDNIGHT—**. 112p. $10.95.
□ Scalapino, Leslie. **Objects in the Terrifying Tense
    Longing from Taking Place**. 88p. $9.95.
□ Seaton, Peter. **The Son Master**. 64p. $5.
□ Sherry, James. **Popular Fiction**. 84p. $6.
□ Silliman, Ron. **The New Sentence**. 200p. $10.
□ Silliman, Ron. **N/O**. 112p. $10.95.
□ Smith, Rod. **Music or Honesty**. 96p. $12.95
□ Smith, Rod. **Protective Immediacy**. 96p. $9.95
□ Stefans, Brian Kim. **Free Space Comix**. 96p. $9.95
□ Tarkos, Christophe. **Ma Langue est Poétique—Selected Works**. 96p. $12.95.
□ Templeton, Fiona. **Cells of Release**. 128p. with photographs. $13.95.
□ Templeton, Fiona. **YOU—The City**. 150p. $11.95.
□ Torres, Edwin. **The All-Union Day of the Shock Worker**. 112 p. $10.95.
□ Tysh, Chris. **Cleavage**. 96p. $11.95.
□ Ward, Diane. **Human Ceiling**. 80p. $8.95.
□ Ward, Diane. **Relation**. 64p. $7.50.
□ Watson, Craig. **Free Will**. 80p. $9.95.
□ Watten, Barrett. **Progress**. 122p. $7.50.
□ Weiner, Hannah. **We Speak Silent**. 76 p. $9.95
□ Weiner, Hannah. **Page**. 136 p. $12.95
□ Wellman, Mac. **Miniature**. 112 p. $12.95
□ Wellman, Mac. **Strange Elegies**. 96 p. $12.95
□ Wolsak, Lissa. **Pen Chants**. 80p. $9.95.
□ Yasusada, Araki. **Doubled Flowering:
    From the Notebooks of Araki Yasusada**. 272p. $14.95.

ROOF BOOKS are published by
Segue Foundation • 300 Bowery • New York, NY 10012
Visit our website at **seguefoundation.com**

ROOF BOOKS are distributed by
SMALL PRESS DISTRIBUTION
1341 Seventh Avenue • Berkeley, CA. 94710-1403.
Phone orders: 800-869-7553
spdbooks.org